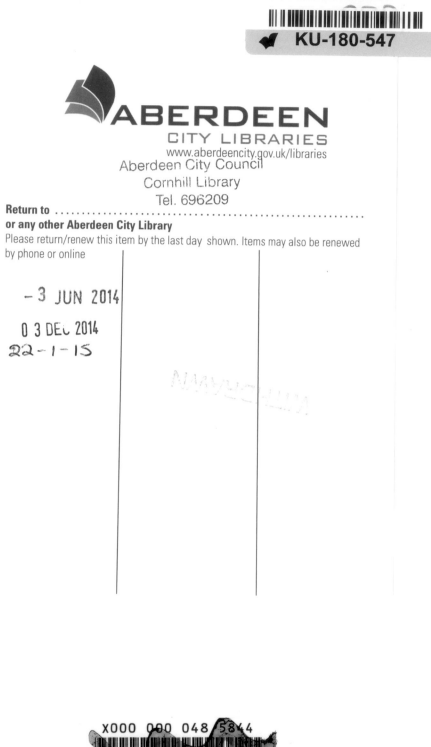

A HOME IN THE COUNTRY

During the Second World War, some 3 million people, most of them children, were evacuated from British towns and cities due to the danger of German air attacks; many were sent to the countryside, but some were sent to Canada, America, Australia, New Zealand and South Africa. A testimony to the resilience of the human spirit and the utter ingenuity of childhood, this heartbreaking tale explores the darker side of the British evacuation during the Second World War and is a testament to youthful resourcefulness and the will to survive.

A HOME IN THE COUNTRY

A HOME IN THE COUNTRY

by

Sheelagh Mawe

Magna Large Print Books
Long Preston, North Yorkshire,
BD23 4ND, England.

British Library Cataloguing in Publication Data.

Mawe, Sheelagh
    A home in the country.

    A catalogue record of this book is
    available from the British Library

    ISBN   978-0-7505-3864-0

First published in Great Britain in 2013 by Robert Hale Limited

Copyright © Sheelagh Mawe 2013

Cover illustration by arrangement with Robert Hale Ltd.

Published in Large Print 2014 by arrangement with
Robert Hale Limited

Magna Large Print is an imprint of Library Magna Books Ltd.

Printed and bound in Great Britain by
T.J. (International) Ltd., Cornwall, PL28 8RW

Dedicated to the thousands of individuals
who spent part, or most, of their
childhood in foster homes.
Hey, you survived!

PROLOGUE

Just as a daily traveller on a familiar highway may occasionally find it necessary, due perhaps to roadworks or an accident, to make a detour in order to arrive safely at their destination, so too are there unexpected events that interrupt the course of a life, some causing a mere ripple, others a disruption so complete that a return to what went before is no longer possible.

And many times, some of the most extraordinary detours one encounters in life begin to take shape under such ordinary circumstances that it is only with hindsight that one can pinpoint their beginning.

Certainly, such was the case for my brother, James, and myself when, many years – better make that decades – after the fact, we attempted to reconstruct our first knowledge of the impending detour sprawling ahead in our young lives – a subject which, without ever quite knowing why, we had always avoided. The only clear memory we could agree upon was one that took place on an unusually sunny afternoon at our home in England. The year was 1940...

ONE

...And we were sitting at the tea table silently watching our mother's hands busy among the teacups. The ritual was always the same: first a little milk was poured into each cup, then a carefully measured teaspoon of sugar – it was, after all, rationed – and then the tea.

The thing that set that particular teatime apart from all the others in our joint memory was the fact that Mummy had been talking. More to the point, she had been talking in a quick and unusually breathless manner whereas, normally, she remained silent and preoccupied until her task was complete and the full cups carefully passed around the table.

She began by saying that she had the most marvellous news ever for us. 'It's your turn now to be refugees,' she beamed, 'and you are going to be evacuated all the way to America! Isn't that exciting?'

James and I exchanged glances.

Not pausing for our response, or even to catch her breath, Mummy hurried on to say, 'It will only be for a little while, darlings. Just until this wretched war is over and England back the way it was before that wicked man, Hitler, started dropping his disgusting bombs all over the place.'

From the way she looked at us, with smiling eyes and raised eyebrows, we knew she expected us to be thrilled at this news but actually, we were a bit suspicious. That was because we'd heard her talk in just such a breathless manner before – though never at teatime – and had noticed that things said at such times, all things that promised amazing results for lucky little children, almost always turned out to be rather unpleasant.

Certainly, the first day of school for each of us had been too awful for words. Same with rushing to our dug-out air raid shelter at the bottom of the garden in the middle of the night when the sirens started their ghastly wailing and the bombs began to fall. And what about all the excitement every time we had to visit the doctor? Take medicine? Be inoculated? We couldn't remember a single event ever bringing the expected magical results, nor worth the sweeties we were promised if we were good sports and didn't cry.

Another puzzling thing our mother seemed to have quite forgotten in her excitement that particular day was that whenever there had been talk in the past of our being evacuated, she had always said that the very idea of little children being separated from their parents and packed off to live with complete strangers, goodness only knew where, simply appalled her.

'You only have to look at all the poor little Londoners evacuated to this village to see what a disastrous idea it is,' she had said. 'Otherwise why are they running away in droves, all of them trying to find their way back to London?'

'Where is America?' James asked, somewhat tentatively.

'I should have thought at age six, James, you'd know where America is,' Daddy growled from his chair by the wireless where he'd gone to sit, teacup and evening paper in hand, in readiness for the sound of Big Ben's chimes announcing the six o'clock news from the BBC. 'It's a country on the other side of the Atlantic Ocean, for God's sake.'

'Yes!' Mummy agreed quickly, worried, as always, that Daddy would fly into one of his rages because we children didn't know things he thought we should. 'And what an exciting and wonderful country it is!'

Unlike most children of that era whose earliest lessons consisted of nursery rhymes and good manners, ours had had more to do with learning to be very careful of what was said in the presence of our father. He had a violent temper and when he lost it he shouted obscene swear words – words Mummy warned us never, under any circumstances, to repeat – and hit any one of us that

13

got in his way.

It will come, then, as no surprise to learn that neither James nor I liked our father at all although we knew it was expected of us. Sister Theresa, my kindergarten teacher at the convent school James and I attended, had once become very angry – livid, actually – when, after telling the class it was their duty to love our Father in heaven, I had replied that I'd try although I didn't like the one at home one bit. Sister was deeply shocked at my words and said I must pray and ask God to forgive me for saying such a wicked thing.

Mummy elaborated further. 'America is a huge and very beautiful country!'

'Bigger than England?' James asked.

'Good gracious me, yes. Much bigger. And the best part about it is that it's far, far away. Too far for that wicked Hitler to drop his nasty bombs.'

'How will we get there, then?' James asked. 'We won't have enough petrol will we?'

Mummy laughed. 'You don't need cars or even trains or buses to go to America, silly. To go to America you get on a lovely big ship – bigger than twenty houses put together, I should say – and you stay on it for about a week while it goes all the way across the Atlantic Ocean. Just imagine that! My goodness, won't that be fun?'

Again, would it? The more excited Mummy became, the more dubious I felt and I asked,

'Where will you be, then?'

On a deep breath that almost wavered, Mummy answered, 'Well, you see, darling, mummies and daddies aren't allowed to travel just now – because of the war, you know – just children. And, of course, your father must stay to go to business and I must stay to look after him. My goodness, someone must, mustn't they? And your pets! Whatever would become of them if I went away, too?'

I hadn't liked the sound of any of it. Not in the least. The very thought of going away and leaving Mummy alone with Daddy made my throat feel tight. It was one of the reasons I hated going to school. I worried he'd call her names and hit her if I wasn't there to pull on his legs and shout at him to stop.

But at least I only went to school half a day and could look after her the rest of the time. But if I went far away on a big ship to America then heaven only knew what might happen.

I remembered something else that had struck me as very odd at the time, which was that the very morning of which I'm speaking, I'd had my bottom soundly spanked for unlatching the garden gate and crossing the lane to the other side. I reasoned that if I wasn't even allowed to go outside the garden by myself, then how on earth could they expect me to go far, far away to America?

When Mummy found me outside the gate that morning she'd said, 'What a naughty, disobedient little girl you are! You know perfectly well you're not allowed to go outside the garden alone. Whatever got into you?'

'I only went to pick the daisies growing in the hedge opposite,' I'd sobbed. 'You always say you like daisies best of all the flowers. And ... I did look both ways,' I added by way of compensating for my naughtiness.

'That was very thoughtful of you, darling,' Mummy conceded. 'But doing exactly as you're told is the best, and most thoughtful, thing of all. Especially now there's a war on. What if the air raid sirens had gone off and I couldn't find you? I'm sorry, darling, but I'm afraid you're going to have to sit in the corner until you're quite sure you remember that.'

It was useless – unthinkable, actually – to contradict one's parents in those days and if Mummy said going to live in America by ourselves was an exciting and wonderful thing and we were very lucky, then that was that. But I did feel I should remind her that I was still only five, something I didn't readily admit to at the time.

'Actually,' I'd begun, 'I don't think I should like to go to America without you, thank you, Mummy. You see, I rather think I'm a bit too ... um ... small. I mean... I might get lost!'

Once I'd said it, I'd begun to feel somewhat ashamed of myself and my head sank so low it was nearly in my teacup.

I heard the sound of Daddy turning a page of the newspaper, heard Mummy give a big sigh, and then James unwittingly came to my rescue saying, 'I like the bit about the big ship, but how on earth will we manage over there by ourselves? Sarah can't even tie her shoelaces properly yet.'

Both parents started talking at once.

Mummy said, 'Oh, darlings ... how silly of me. I didn't mean you'd be going to America all by yourselves.'

Daddy said, 'Good God, I should say not! You won't be by yourselves on the ship or in America. There will be people to look after you every single minute.'

Looking at me very sternly over the top of both his glasses and the newspaper, he'd added, 'And of course you must go. You don't realize your extreme good fortune. Every child in England would like to go to America just now. Besides, it's your duty. It will be your way of helping the war effort.'

Mummy agreed. 'Yes, and a jolly useful way it will be, too. And as Daddy just told you, you won't be alone. Some very kind, very brave ladies are going to escort you and take care of you and all the other lucky little children who will be travelling with you. Children your own age for the most part, I expect. And then, when you get off the ship

17

in New York–'

'I thought you said we got off in America,' James interrupted.

'I did, darling. You will. New York is a big city at the very edge of America. It has lots of huge, tall buildings so high they seem to scrape the sky; that's what people call them, skyscrapers. Wait till you see!'

'Is everything in America big, then?' James wondered.

'Yes, darling. Huge. Now, when you get off the ship your escort will take you to a hostel. A hostel is rather like a hotel. That is well, it's a big house with lots of rooms called dormitories just for children. And that's where you will stay until foster parents can be found for you and then–'

'What are foster parents?' James asked.

Mummy sighed. 'Darling, please. You really must stop interrupting. I was just getting to that. Foster parents are ... well, they're temporary parents. Dear, kind people who will look after you and pretend to be your mother and father until–'

What? A pretend mother? I tumbled out of my chair to throw myself at Mummy and tell her I didn't need a pretend mother, thank you very much. I said, 'Why would I when I have my very own proper one?'

Mummy gave me a quick, reassuring hug. 'And always will. But now back to your chair, please, darling. You haven't finished your bread and butter. You didn't fold your napkin. And you didn't ask to be excused, did you?'

Reluctantly I got back in my chair while Mummy went on talking. 'By the time you arrive I'm quite sure a lovely home will have been found for you. Perhaps, if you're very lucky, a home in the country. Think of that! No more hateful air raid sirens getting you out of bed to run to that nasty, damp old shelter – elbows off the table please, James. No more smelly old gas masks to trundle with you everywhere you go. No more bombs crashing down. No more rationing. All the eggs and milk and meat and vegetables growing children need. And sweeties galore! Just like here before the war!'

Strangely, I wasn't that interested in the sweeties just at that moment because such an awful thought had popped into my head that I interrupted Mummy, even though I knew it was rude. 'But Mummy, what if the war goes on forever and ever?' I asked.

'Impossible,' Daddy snorted.

Mummy agreed. 'No fear of that. Our Mr Churchill simply wouldn't put up with it. You'll see, it will all be over in a few months. Perhaps a year at the very outside. Just until we do away with that wicked man, Hitler, and England is safe again.'

I remember I started to cry then, which was upsetting in itself as I had prided myself on having outgrown such a babyish habit. But really, it seemed perfectly obvious to me that if England wasn't safe for children then it couldn't possibly be safe for adults either.

'But what if a bomb falls on you or the Germans come while we're away? We might never find you,' I sobbed. 'Then whatever should we do?'

Mummy told me not to worry. 'Leave that up to your father and me,' she said. 'We know what's best and we'll be quite safe, you'll see. Meantime, you are to be a good girl and finish your tea. And for heaven's sake, smile please. Nobody likes long, weepy faces.'

But by then I'd had quite enough of trying to be good and more than enough of adult logic, thank you. Raising my voice to maximum volume, I shouted, 'I hate being little! And I hate being made to go on a ridiculous journey to America! Why can't you understand that if you'll be quite safe here, then so should we? I don't want to be a refugee! And I don't want a pretend mother either! Most of all, I hate bloody old Hitler! I shan't go!'

I stopped, both pleased and horrified at the shocked expressions on both parents' faces. And then I started crying all over again, every bit as shocked as they, and I left my chair once again to throw myself at Mummy.

'I didn't mean all of it,' I choked between sobs, 'and I do want to be good and do as I'm told. It's just that I don't think sending us to

America while this beastly war is going on is a good idea. How do you know our ship won't be torpedoed and sunk like the ones we hear about on the news? And how do you know we won't be captured by the Germans and sent to a prison camp? Or starved? Or that the foster parents you spoke of will be truly kind? I think it would be so much better, and safer, if we all just stayed happily together here in England and be blowed with bloody old Hitler and his stupid bombs.'

Mummy stroked my hair and told me I was her good, brave little girl. 'We must all do things we'd rather not when there's a war on,' she consoled. 'After all, drastic times require drastic measures. And, you'll see, parents really do know what's best for their children. What we want for you is a safe and carefree childhood and heaven knows it simply isn't possible in England at the moment.'

Once James and I had resurrected the memory of that long-ago teatime, it became increasingly easy to remember, in surprising detail, what followed and, once started, we seemed unable to stop. For one thing, the carefully structured routines of our household changed abruptly as Mummy busied herself with all the criteria necessary for our departure. Some meals were delayed or by-passed altogether, while items on her grocery list were forgotten, and bath and bedtime were often late. Much more interesting from James' and my point of view, however, were the days we were kept home from school altogether in order to accompany our parents on necessary journeys to the Foreign Office in London for the all-important passports.

While those journeys were eagerly looked forward to by us children, they were a great worry to our parents since London was no longer considered a safe place to visit. Mummy, in particular, worried about air raids, while Daddy obsessed over having enough petrol for the journey and getting home before dark because of the blackout and not being allowed to use the car headlights.

On one ghastly occasion it did get dark before we got home and Daddy started getting all worked up about it, shouting that it was all Mummy's fault. Sitting behind him in the back seat of the car, I saw one of his hands let go of the steering wheel and bunch itself into a fist, ready to punch the side of her face, when a full moon came out from behind a cloud and he could see quite well.

'Thank you, moon!' Mummy exclaimed, before going on to explain to James and me that the moon we were looking at was the very same moon that shone in America and every time she saw it while we were away, she would blow it kisses for us, and when we saw it we could blow it kisses for her and

Daddy and that way we wouldn't seem so very far apart after all.

Daddy stopped his shouting at those words but James and I, while dimly understanding they were meant to cheer us up, wished she hadn't said anything at all. For rather than comforting us, they made us want to ask, 'How far is far away?'

London most definitely was not the nice, exciting place James and I remembered from our few pre-war visits. The first time we drove in we were all quite horrified at what we saw. Over and over Daddy said, 'Good God!' and 'Bloody outsiders!' While between gasps and moans, Mummy said, 'Blast those Germans! Look what they've done. Now do you see why it's best for you to go to America, darlings? Look, so many houses quite gone, all reduced to rubble. And look at the sand bags! And the queues! Why, they must stretch for miles. Fancy having to wait for hours on end for a wretched potato or a measly ounce of tea. Just think how lucky we are to live in the country with our own little bit of garden to grow a few spuds and keep the odd chicken.'

The Foreign Office with its blacked-out windows was not at all the exciting place we had expected from its important-sounding name either. Everyone there seemed harried and disagreeable and we had to queue for hours.

When it finally came time for James and

me to be inoculated, even Mummy looked cross. 'Crying is quite out of the question,' she warned. 'The hospitals in London are filled to bursting with children – children a good bit younger than either of you, please note – with missing arms and legs and goodness only knows what else, and none of them are crying. Not a single one.'

In what seemed no time at all there came a morning when we were wakened in the pre-dawn by Mummy's voice chirping, 'Wake up, you lucky little sleepyheads! Today's the day you set off to discover America. Just like Christopher Columbus!'

Oh, dear ... I knew Mummy wanted us to be thrilled and if we couldn't manage that to at least be good sports, but really, it was so awful having to pretend all the time that I said, 'I think being a small child is the worst possible thing that can happen to anyone and I wish that stupid Christopher Columbus had stayed at home and learned to mind his own business.'

I finished my outburst, adding, 'When I grow up I shall never go anywhere. I shall stay in my own little home always and only do things that make me happy.'

'I quite understand,' Mummy said, 'but meantime there is a war on and you and James do have your train to catch to the coast. Now please hurry with your dressing or we'll have Daddy ranting and raving all the way to London, God forbid.'

Of course, Daddy ranted and raved all the way to London anyway, it not being in his nature to pass up such a splendid opportunity. He ranted because it was still dark and raining hard and he couldn't find the blacked-out train station. When he finally did, he began raving because there were so many men in uniform dashing about in the gloom with their kit bags looking for their trains, he couldn't find ours.

He had just worked himself up to the most obscene words in his repertoire when a stocky, harried-looking woman in a uniform with a badge on the front of her hat planted herself in front of him and said, 'For God's sake, control yourself, sir, and follow me.'

She led us to a dreary, poorly lit room where many families such as ours were queuing up at a table at which more uniformed ladies were checking names and passports and tickets against lengthy lists.

Whilst tying luggage-label name tags to the top buttonholes of James' and my coats, the harried-looking woman told us that we were to call her Escort. 'I shan't put up with any nonsense from either of you,' she warned. 'I am, after all, responsible for many other children besides yourselves. Just remember there is a war on.'

Turning to our parents she instructed

them to take us along to the train at platform four, and find carriage number twelve. 'You are to say your goodbyes briskly and leave the train at once,' she advised. 'I can't put up with a lot of tears. Bad for morale, you know. Remind yourselves there's a war on.'

I fully expected Daddy to start calling her the ghastly names he called Mummy but ever since she'd told him to control himself he'd been strangely silent. It occurred to me then that if only Mummy would talk to him the way Escort had, he might learn to behave himself a bit better.

For all that, I didn't think the Escort woman was one bit nice and I tugged on Mummy's coat sleeve to tell her so. 'I don't want to go to America with her,' I complained. 'You said she'd be quite wonderful but she's not. She's horrid.'

'I'm quite sure she's really very charming,' Mummy said, trying to reassure me. 'It's just that she has a lot to cope with at the moment and it's up to you two to help by doing exactly as you're told every single minute and– Look! There's carriage twelve and, just as I thought, filled to bursting with children your age!'

Daddy lifted our suitcases up to the over-head rack – both James and I remembered how taken we had been with our little new suitcases – sat on the edge of the seat and said, 'Right you are then. Time for Mummy and me to run along. Escort will be here presently to look after you. James, I expect you to be very brave, old chap. Do as you're told, look after your sister and above all, remember you are an Englishman. Sarah, this is not the time for a long face. Remember your duty. It is to smile. You're the luckiest little girl in the world and you'll be back in no time at all, speaking like a Yank, I expect.' He shook James' hand, kissed the top of my head, then tripped and fell and swore loudly while descending to the platform.

Mummy took his place on the edge of the seat and, after much rummaging in her handbag, produced two small chocolate bars. 'Look, darlings!' she exclaimed. 'Real chocolate! I've been saving our sweetie ration for weeks and weeks so you could have these on the train.'

In those days chocolate was, of course, an almost forgotten luxury, but that day it didn't seem the least bit appealing. Both of us remembered not being able to imagine eating it at all because our tummies ached and our throats felt tight and I, for one, was sure I wouldn't be able to swallow so much as a crumb without being sick.

Mummy began talking again in the quick and breathless manner we had come to distrust. 'Daddy is quite right, you know. You will be coming home in no time at all. Everyone says the war will be over in less than a year. Even Mr Churchill, and he should certainly know!'

I knew perfectly well that I was expected to be brave and agreeable but I couldn't help myself. 'Please, please don't make us go,' I begged. 'Not without you. I'll be ever so good and obedient every single minute and look ... I'll even give you my chocolate bar if only you'll let us stay.'

For a moment, Mummy looked so desperately sad I wished I hadn't said anything but, drawing upon God only knows what reserves of strength, she swallowed hard, gave us a big smile and, hugging us close, said, 'You are the very best children in the world. That's why you are going away. So you'll be happy and safe and when the war is over we can all live quietly in peace. Sit in your seats now, darlings. Be brave! Smile!' And, smiling and waving and blowing kisses, she turned away.

I stood to go with her because in spite of all we'd been told, I'd never really quite come to terms with the reality that she would, or even could, actually go away and leave me behind.

But then, just as she stepped down to the platform, Escort got on, slammed the door shut and the train started to move.

'There we are then!' Escort trilled, clearly determined to be cheerful. 'Are we all smiling? That's the way. Smile and wave goodbye to your mummies and daddies.'

We all turned to wave and smile but it was

hard to find one's own set of parents amongst so many others, the more so since it was still dark outside. Many eyes overflowed with tears, and rain slashed against the windows. We stood to see better.

Escort didn't like that one bit. 'In your seats now, children,' she ordered. Then louder, 'Sit down!' And finally, resorting to the sarcasm that has warped so many an English child's mind, 'I suppose someone did tell you there's a war on? That being the case, you are to obey instantly. Right, now we will sing a song.'

Blowing a note into a little mouth organ she'd taken from her pocket, she said, 'Yes! Yes! Nothing like a song to cheer us along. How many of you know, "Pack Up Your Troubles in Your Old Kit Bag"? That's a jolly one. No one? Good gracious me! Wrong war, perhaps? Well, what about the Blue-birds? You know, the ones that fly over the White Cliffs of Dover? Ah! That's better. Yes, Sarah, what is it?'

'My mother says the bluebirds song is the soppiest song she ever heard,' I said, just as smug as could be.

'Your mother also said you were to do as you were told, didn't she? Therefore, YOU WILL SING!'

TWO

Just as Escort was not at all the kind, charming woman Mummy had foretold, neither was our cabin on the ship the dear, cosy little place she had described in another of her monologues. Rather, it was hot, stuffy and dark and because, that first day, we could not find the light switch, we couldn't see where to hang up our coats and hats as Escort had instructed.

Tentatively we groped our way towards our bunks and perched on the edges of them – James on the upper – since the small area of usable floor space was taken up by our suitcases and a large chair that refused to be moved. James had exerted great effort in the attempt until, 'No wonder,' he panted, studying it at close range from a kneeling position, 'Some silly ass has bolted it to the floor!'

The stupidity of anyone doing such an extraordinary thing silenced our sobs temporarily and our attention drifted to the well-lit corridor outside our cabin where we could see our fellow travellers running back and forth to each other's cabins with what appeared to us an enviable light-heartedness. Was it because they were older than us, we wondered, that they didn't seem the least bit unhappy at leaving their mothers, or intimidated by Escort?

One of the children, a big husky girl, shouted, 'Look out! Here comes old Escort!' And sure enough, we could hear her talking. Worse, she was talking about us!

She was asking if anyone had seen the little ones. 'No? Well, where are the naughty little things then?'

Stopping outside our door, her hand reached in and turned on the light. 'Goodness gracious me!' she exclaimed. 'Here they are! And sitting in the dark if you don't mind!

'You're going to have to do better than this, my dears,' she sniffed. 'Long, weepy faces simply aren't good enough. There is a war on you know and it is your duty to be cheerful and do as you're told! Now take off those hats and coats immediately. Hang them up! Open your suitcases!'

James clambered down from the top bunk and Escort told him she was going to rely on him to see that little Sarah did as she was told. 'After all,' she said, 'I can't be expected to cope with one lazy, sulky little girl when I have so many other children depending on me, now can I?'

She was interrupted by a loud thud and the entire ship giving a mighty shudder.

'We're off!' she crowed. 'What fun!'

I strained against the back of my bunk

with all my might and screamed at Escort to make the ship stop so I could get off. 'I don't want to go without my mother,' I howled. 'I won't!'

James told me to shut up. 'You know jolly well the ship won't stop and you can't get off,' he said. Turning to Escort he tried to explain that I wasn't really a lazy, sulky little girl at all. 'She's just–'

Escort interrupted him. How rude. 'It's quite all right, James,' she said with a sniff. 'I understand. Sarah's a baby, that's all. You'll have to do everything for her, I expect. Ah, well–'

'I am not a baby!' I interrupted with a great burst of indignation that temporarily stemmed my tears. 'I shall be six next birthday!'

To prove my point, I wiggled a front tooth with my tongue, 'Look, I've even got another loose tooth!'

Escort was not impressed. 'Charming,' she murmured, averting her eyes. 'Then you should certainly know how to take off your coat and hat. And it shouldn't be too much to ask that you hang up your clothes. Are you quite sure you're going to be six?'

To prove I was, I took off my hat and coat. Escort moved the suitcases so she could open the little wardrobe and I hung them up and then she handed me the rest of my clothing to put away.

'Perhaps you're right,' she said as we worked together. 'Perhaps you are nearly six. Now the minute you finish putting away your clothes I want you both to wash your faces and hands and then wait outside in the corridor where I can see you because we shall be going to dinner presently. Won't that be fun?'

Not if she said so, it wouldn't. For even at that early stage of our journey it had become quite obvious to both James and myself that it wasn't just our mother, but all adults, who were seriously misinformed as to what was fun and exciting to a child.

Further, when the dining room proved to be the source of the nauseating stench of vegetable soup that permeated the entire ship – a soup which, interestingly, looked exactly the same when sicked-up on the floor as it did in a bowl – the dining room became for us a thrice daily trek to what, in modern parlance, would undoubtedly be called Vomit City.

Escort was furious about our constant sickness. Flinging down her napkin that first night, she muttered, 'Really... Children this age... Far too young... Come along then. Quickly, quickly...'

James was sick twice more after Escort returned us to our cabin. He cleaned it up as best he could with the towels hanging by our little sink but then couldn't think what to do with the towels.

And all the while he was busy being sick and worrying about the towels, I had been struggling to get my lovely pink pullover – the one Mummy had knit for me using the very last of our clothing coupons for the wool – over my head, and I couldn't. It was stuck. It was pinching my ears, the neck buttons were tangled in my hair, and it simply would not come off.

Before he was sick, James had tried to help but couldn't manage either and said I must go and find Escort.

For him to have even suggested such a stupid thing made me realize how truly useless he was going to be and I came up with my own plan to deal with the situation: I would simply put my arms back in the sleeves, pull it back down and leave it on all night.

Escort would never know because we had to wear our life jackets on top of everything at all times anyway, and if she did come in to say goodnight – she'd said she would but I hoped she'd forget – I'd just pull the blankets up to my eyes and pretend to be asleep.

And since James clearly wasn't able, or willing, to help me in other useful ways, I thought I might just as well leave my shoes and socks on as well. That way I wouldn't have all the bother of tying the laces properly in the morning.

Like adults the world over, Escort was of the opinion that fresh air was good for children and hustled her charges outside at every opportunity.

After only one outing, James and I agreed that fresh air was just one more thing adults were quite wrong about. Particularly the variety found at sea, which was so fierce it blew us off our feet, sent huge waves crashing over the railing, and whipped away anything and everything we were foolish enough to carry in our hands. It was also bitterly cold and sent us to cower in corners whenever Escort looked the other way.

All of these discomforts paled, however, when compared to the dreaded lifeboat-drill ordeal that we were forced to attend at odd times during the day no matter how seasick we might be or how rough and cold the weather.

Actually, lifeboat drills were quite frightening events at that time because no one was ever quite sure if they were real or practice. News had quickly circulated that two ships in our convoy had already been torpedoed and sunk. From our hiding place in an alcove near the dining room, James and I overheard our escort tell another that she believed one of them had been packed to overflowing with little refugees just like ours.

'Just think of it,' she'd gasped. 'All those little mites at the bottom of the sea! Think of their parents hearing the news! Ghastly! Tragic!'

At lifeboat drills sailors shouted and waved flags and blew whistles, and how on earth we were supposed to stay together – we'd been told we must stay together no matter what – and get to the lifeboat if a torpedo hit our ship, we couldn't imagine. We even wondered if we'd manage to find 'our' lifeboat in time.

We never did.

'As ghastly as all this is,' James complained one morning while we awaited the breakfast summons, 'the absolute worst part of all this evacuation rubbish is having to look after you,' his lip curled, 'a girl. At least if you were a boy I wouldn't have to brush your hair every day and you'd have stopped crying by now.'

'It's not because I'm a girl I can't stop crying, you silly fool!' I howled. 'It's because even though I know Mummy isn't here, I still wake up every morning expecting to see her. And then I can't get the tangles out of my hair and you're being hateful. And then I'm being sick and then we get lost and Escort shouts at us. It gives me a horrid empty feeling inside and I don't feel safe and that's what makes me cry.'

James remained unconvinced. 'Even Escort feels sorry for me,' he glowered. 'She says you never answer when she speaks to you. She even says you're the naughtiest little girl on the ship.'

I burst into fresh tears. 'That's what she tells everyone,' I sniffled, 'and it's not true. I'm not naughty. I don't answer when she speaks to me because the lump in my throat is so huge I can never make words go around it.'

In my opinion, the worst part about being on the ship, apart from James' unkindness and stupidity, was that it wouldn't, not even for a second, stop tossing and heaving and that's why I was so relentlessly, disgustingly sick.

Actually, odd as it may sound, it was fortunate I was sick one particular morning because that was how we met Alf and our journey took a huge turn for the better. Alf was a sailor and he was the dearest, kindest man we ever met. One that I fervently wished I could exchange for my own father.

'Watcha tryin' to do, eh?' he'd laughed, emptying a bucket of water on the horrid mess I'd made and swabbing it overboard before anyone else could see it. 'Make me work 'arder?'

Alf laughed at all the things that terrified us. This included submarines, torpedoes, big waves, lifeboat drills, Hitler, ship's food and, best of all, Escort.

It was Alf who explained that the reason the awful empty feeling went with me everywhere and I couldn't stop crying wasn't because I was naughty at all, but because I was 'omesick.

'Bein' 'omesick,' he told me, 'is somefing what 'appens to everyone – everyone wiv 'alf a 'eart, that is – the first time they go away from 'ome.'

'Did it happen to you?' I asked.

'Crikey, yes,' he said. 'Cried two weeks straight, I did, first time I come on board. Captain said 'e never saw the likes, me bein' all growed up an' all, but s'truth. Couldn't stop no matter 'ow 'ard I tried.'

I felt ever so much better after he told me that and thought perhaps 'omesickness was something Escort must have forgotten about because she was so old. Or more likely, perhaps, because she didn't even have half a heart.

One evening in the lounge, Escort said, 'We shan't be singing songs around the piano this evening, children. We are going to write letters home to our parents instead. Won't that be fun?'

Of course not.

Escort passed out pens and paper but because I had never written a letter before, I had no idea how to even start. Escort came to help. Sitting down opposite me, she picked up a pen, stifled a sigh, and waited. I did the same.

Finally, 'Well?' Escort coaxed.

'Tell her…'

Escort frowned, 'Tell who?'

'My mother.'

'And what about your father?'

'Yes… I suppose… My father, too.'

'Sarah, if we are writing this letter to your mother and father, then we must begin it with "Dear Mummy and Daddy," or how can they be expected to know who it's for?'

'Dear Mummy and Daddy,' I said hastily, then stopped, uncertain again as to what should come next.

I looked away from Escort – actually from the badge on her hat, which was what I always studied when she was at close quarters – and down at the paper. The blank paper.

'Really, Sarah,' Escort sighed, 'what is it you want to tell Mummy and Daddy?'

Taking a deep breath, I began. 'Please tell them I hate the ship. It's not at all the fun Mummy said it would be. It's very frightening. Especially when we have to go on deck in the middle of the night because of the sirens and the submarines. And the food is nasty. Soup every day. I'm sick all the time and I don't want to be here. I can't stop crying for a minute and I do so wish they had let me stay at home where I would have been so much better off, as well as much safer. And … I'm 'omesick as well as the other sick and I can't get the lovely pink pullover she knitted

39

for me over my head no matter how hard I try. I just do so wish they had listened to me...'

'Sarah! Really!' Escort gasped. 'You mustn't worry your parents with things like that. Good heavens, there's a war on, child. You must tell them how well and happy you are and the fun you have singing songs around the piano every evening. And about the stories we read. And then what about all the lovely food we have to eat with fresh oranges for pudding some nights? My goodness, they'd certainly want to hear about that.'

Again the pen waited.

'But I'm not happy,' I protested. 'And I'm not at all well. I can't stop being sick.'

Escort started writing. She read out loud as her pen moved across the paper. 'I am very well and happy. Last night we sang songs around the piano and–'

I interrupted, suddenly knowing exactly what to say to make them happy. 'Please tell them that Alf says soon's this bloody war's over wiv he's coming to fetch us and take us 'ome. Alf says–'

Escort wasn't writing. Instead, her mouth puffing like that of an angry dragon, she said, 'What shocking language from such a little girl. And who, pray tell, is Alf?'

'Alf is our friend. He's a sailor. He's very jolly and very brave. He makes us laugh. He says down with the 'uns and bloody old 'itler.'

Escort sniffed. 'I don't think your parents want to hear that you have been spending your time with a common sailor, Sarah. Least of all a Cockney sailor.'

She started to write, speaking the words as she went along, 'I hope you and Daddy are well, too.'

She handed me the pen, turning the paper to face me. 'Now write, "love Sarah",' she instructed.

Studying the floor, I wondered if love should start with a big 'L' or a little one? I made a big one in the air for her to see. 'Like that?' I asked.

Escort snatched back pen and paper, wrote 'love', and left me to write my name. To be quite certain Mummy would know it was really me writing the letter, I wrote all of them, first, middle, and last. And then, even though Escort hadn't said I could and might be cross, I drew a circle for the moon and filled it with Xs, trusting that Escort was far too old to know that Xs stood for kisses.

Coming upon us one frigid day, huddled in a corner out of the wind, Alf danced a jig and said, 'We'll be in New York first thing in the morning, mates!'

'Is it nice there?' James asked. 'We've been a bit worried we might not like it at all.'

'Blimey, yes, New York's nice,' Alf said. 'New York's a bit of all right is what it is. In't no war goin' on there, see. No bombs. No blackout. No rubble. No sand bags. No bloody rationin'. New York's all about bright lights and pretty girls and lovely grub everywhere you go. You'll like it, see if you don't.'

In the lounge that same evening, Escort said, 'There will be no singing around the piano tonight, children. And no stories. Instead you are to go straight to your cabins, pack up your belongings, make sure you have everything, and then you are to take baths. Won't that be fun?'

Hardly. Not with me still unable to get my lovely pink jumper over my head, it wouldn't. I hurried off to find Alf.

For once he was at a loss. 'It wouldn't be proper, like, for me to take it off and 'ave you runnin' about the ship in your vest, now would it?' he asked.

Then he remembered there was a lovely young lady on the other side of the ship and off we went to find her.

The lovely young lady accompanied me back to the entrance of our bathroom, gave my jumper a few good tugs and off it came. And a good thing, too, we decided. It was very grubby and stained with sick and we couldn't imagine what Mummy would think if she saw it. She'd be too shocked to think at all, was what we decided.

I was still very put out about taking a bath, though. I'd never had to take my clothes off in front of people I didn't know and what if they stared at my bottom? Mummy always said that bottoms are very private and were to be kept covered at all times. I thought perhaps I wouldn't take a bath at all but say that I had.

Escort caught me sidling away from the door of the wash area, snatched off my clothes and plopped me down next to a big girl in a tub of very hot, very salty water. The big girl was furious at having 'a baby' like me thrust in beside her. She was so angry she stood up to get out and although I knew it was rude to stare, I was interested to see that she looked just like me with no clothes on except that she had freckles everywhere and her bottom was as red as the meat I used to see hanging on hooks in the village butcher shop.

Thinking that if my bottom were that red I would certainly want to know about it, I told the girl about hers and that made her furious all over again. So furious, in fact, that she leaned over the tub and smacked the side of my face.

Escort leaned in and smacked the other side, saying, 'Not only are you the naughtiest little girl on the ship but you are quite definitely the rudest as well.'

My face stung so badly my eyes watered

and I couldn't see either of them properly but I didn't care. If, in spite of all my efforts to be good, rude and naughty was how they saw me, then I might as well be rude and naughty. Sticking out my tongue, I heaved great armfuls of water in their general direction and served them right.

The next morning as we were finishing breakfast, Escort stood up and announced, 'We'll be getting off the ship within the hour, children! Make sure you have everything.'

And wasn't it odd? The moment she said that, James and I decided that the hated ship was really rather a nice place after all and we'd rather stay on it. We hurried off to find Alf.

We told him we'd come up with a change of plans. 'What if,' we said, 'you hide us somewhere so that we can go back to England with you? That way you won't have all the bother of coming to fetch us when the war is over.'

We went on to explain that we'd be as quiet as mice and nobody need ever know we were there. All he had to do was bring us a little food when no one was looking and the war was bound to be over by the time we got all the way back to England.

'Get on wiv you!' Alf said. 'You've come all this way, mates, you've got to give it a go!'

Perhaps he wasn't such a wonderful friend after all.

44

Before we knew it we were off the ship and in a bus on our way to the hostel place Mummy had told us about. Once there James was put in a dormitory just for boys on one side of the building and I was put in one for girls on the opposite side. What shocked me the most about all that was, although I'd never liked James the least little bit, when he turned away to go to the boys' side, I wanted to call after him to stay with me, or else let me go with him. Anything rather than stay with the soppy-looking group of small girls all staring at me from one end of the corridor. I felt awkward and shy and longed, above all, for the comforting presence of my mother. I turned away quickly so no one would notice how much I wanted to cry.

As it turned out, dormitories were nothing more than huge rooms filled with beds and everything in them was white: the beds, the bed clothes, the curtains. Even the ladies who looked after us wore white, shoes and stockings included.

When I first realized that that big room had not one speck of colour anywhere, or anything else that looked the least bit friendly, the awful, empty feeling came back in my tummy and I thought, Surely I'm not going to be 'omesick all over again, am I? Really, I just can't. It's too awful. But, oh, dear ... I do so wish Mummy was here beside me. Or Alf ... or even James...

While we had been waiting to get off the ship and staring up at the Statue of Liberty and the tall, grey skyscraper things that seemed to blot out the sky, James and I both had the overwhelming sense that any one of those tall, tall buildings could easily topple and come crashing down on top of us. We were just deciding where we should hide when Alf turned up and made everything seem safe again. He was laughing and he said, 'Go on then, mates! Give it a go! It in't 'alf as bad as it looks. And don't forget, soon's this bloody lot's over wiv, I'm comin' lookin' for you.'

Dear Alf. He was a good friend after all.

All the children in our group were quite delighted when we learned that Escort hadn't come to the hostel with us. Instead, the ladies in white who were called Matrons were to look after us. Speaking in a manner that baffled yet intrigued us, they said things like, 'Quit that bawling!' And, 'You don't eat you don't grow. Then what's your mudders and fadders gonna say, huh?'

One of them actually thought my name was honey! She said, 'Let's go, Honey. Time to eat.'

'My name isn't Honey,' I gasped. 'It's Sarah. Honey is something bees make. You spread it on bread. Like jam...'

The lady laughed so hard she had to sit

46

down. 'Oh, honey,' she wheezed, 'I know your name's not honey. It's just you're cute and sweet. Here, anybody cute as you gets called honey. You get it? Honey's sweet, right?'

'Oh...' I said, somewhat doubtfully.

'Tell you what,' the lady went on. 'If it'll make you feel better, I'll call you Sarah-Honey. Is that gonna be OK?'

I said that would be all right. Actually, I quite liked it.

All day and every day the Matrons kept telling us what lucky little kids – children, we quickly learned, were called kids in America – we were to have escaped the blitz and crossed the Atlantic Ocean safely in terrible times like these. 'Although,' they went on to mutter among themselves, 'the way those British pack up their kids and send them away like they was last week's dirty wash beats anything we ever heard tell about.'

Every day at the hostel, children – kids – left to go to their new homes. I remember being very happy to see the hateful girl with the red, freckled bottom leave.

In no time at all James and I were the last of the evacuees left. The matron in charge told us, 'The reason you kids are the last is because we have to find a home that will take the both of you and that's not so easy as finding a place for just the one kid.

'Having to find a Catholic home isn't

helping things either,' she'd gone on.

A final reason Matron gave for us being the last to go was because we had a bad reputation. 'A reputation,' she explained, 'is what people say about you when you are not there to hear them.'

Our reputation was that we were the most uncooperative kids on the ship.

We both thought that was horribly unfair.

Matron said, 'Don't ask me. All I know is what I hear and I don't want to hear no more about it. "Actions speak louder than words" is what I always say.'

At last a day came when Matron announced, 'A home has been found for you two out of state, thank God! I was beginning to think we'd have you here for the duration.'

Right away James wanted to know what 'out of state' meant, but before Matron could answer he thought of another, more interesting, question. 'What kind of car will our foster parents come to fetch us in?' he asked.

'You won't be leaving in a car,' Matron explained. 'That's because out of state means you are going out of New York, the state. I'm going to put you on a train that will take you there. The train conductor will keep an eye on you and see that you get off at the right stop where your foster parents will meet you, maybe with a car, maybe not, and take you to their home from there.'

And, 'No, I don't know who your foster

parents are or what they're like or if they have kids of their own or a home in the country. A lady called Mrs Bennings from an organization that finds homes for orphan kids will be with them to introduce you and you can ask her.'

THREE

When a 'kid' is put on a train by a distracted adult and its destination is a meaningless name, it does not want to arrive. The train becomes a safe cocoon where there is no one to answer to, nothing is expected of you, and the kid's most fervent desire is to travel thus forever.

Certainly, as we relived those far-off days, James and I were unanimous in agreeing that was exactly how we'd felt as we set off on the last leg of our journey, the one in which we'd meet our foster parents, the very thought of whom filled us with dry-mouthed dread. Nobody had to tell us that those people would be around longer than any Escort or Matron, and certainly a lot longer than the kindly, black, Pullman porter, Harvey, in whose temporary care we had been placed.

The very word 'parent', foster or other-wise, meant people who would tell us what to do, what to wear, what to eat and how to behave. But what if, as in the case of our real parents, they decided to pack us off to a place to which we did not want to go? Or what if they were of the Grimm variety? She a witch who cackled; he a giant who craved the blood of an Englishman? What would we, could we, do then?

'I do hope she's kind,' I gulped to James as the train carrying us plunged into a tunnel, 'not like poor little Cinderella's. And I do so hope she's pretty.'

'Who?'

'Our ... you know. Our, um ... stepmother.'

James scowled and seemed to shrink in his already too large, bought-with-growth-in-mind, dark blue blazer.

'Time to go to the dining car, kids,' Harvey called.

'Follow me.'

The dining car? We exchanged uneasy glances. What would be expected of us there? Reluctantly we rose and followed our guide. Oh ... a dining car was a dining room. A dining room on wheels. Fancy that. Was that why it was called a car? But shouldn't it be called a dining carriage since everyone knows trains are made up of carriages, not cars?

'Pick anything you want,' Harvey said, handing us each a menu.

'I'm not hungry,' I said truthfully, pleased that I wouldn't have to admit that I could

50

scarcely read. James surprised me, saying he wasn't hungry either, even though he was then nearly seven and knew perfectly well how to read.

One forearm across his middle to support the elbow of his other arm, the hand of which stroked his chin, Harvey thought about that so long that both James and I, without consultation, adopted his pose and began stroking our chins.

'Tell you what,' Harvey said finally, finished with his thinking and stroking and thereby terminating ours, 'let's just skip everything on that menu except dessert. What say I bring you each a double-dip of chocolate ice cream? Sound good?'

Our eyes widened at the thought and we nodded eagerly. But by the time the ice cream arrived, my mind had wandered back to wicked stepmothers and, after a mouthful or two, I set my spoon aside.

'What shall we do if she's cruel and hits us?' I asked James.

Lost in thoughts of his own and absent-mindedly stirring his ice cream into a soup, James didn't answer.

'If she hits me, you'll have to make her stop,' I told him. 'Daddy said so. It's your job to look after me.'

Before he could reply, Harvey reappeared beside us and studied our barely touched ice cream in the same chin-stroking manner

51

as before.

'It didn't melt, I'd save it for my grand-kids,' he said, shaking his head in sorrow. 'They know what to do with double-dips of chocolate ice cream, believe you me. Come on now, I'll take you back to your seats. We'll be there in a couple more hours.'

Oh, dear ... I turned to James and in a whisper, said, 'What if she makes us eat fish? Or spinach? I know, let's ask Harvey if we can live at his house! He's ever so nice. Almost as nice as Alf. And we'd be very good. We could show him we know how to eat ice cream just like his grandkids and–'

'Shut up,' James growled.

Harvey kept us in our seats until almost all the other passengers had left the platform before leading us, each clinging to one of his hands – those fascinating, pink on the inside hands – off the train.

'Keep your eyes out for a lady in a blue coat,' he told us. 'That's how you'll know who she is, your new stepmom. Her and an-other woman, uh...' he consulted a slip of paper, '...a Mrs Bennings are s'posed to meet you here.'

A blue coat? I didn't want to look for any kind of coat. Especially not one being worn by my new stepmom. It was much more interesting to look at my feet and wonder why, in spite of my reluctance to go places I did not want to go, they always took me there anyway?

'She must have forgotten,' I heard James say after what seemed an age. 'There's not a single blue coat anywhere.'

I felt such a rush of relief I had to hold on extra tight to Harvey's hand while I looked up to see for myself.

'He's right,' I told Harvey gleefully. 'See, no blue coats. Not one. So can we ... um... Well, what if... I mean, would it be all right if we came to live at your house? We'd be ever so good.'

Before he could answer, a tall, anxious-looking woman wearing a black coat came hurrying towards us, talking in what came across as fragments over the hiss and rumble of trains pulling in and out of the platforms to either side of us.

'...Bennings...' her mouth jabbered. '...Kids... British... Late... Couldn't come... Sorry... Really... I... Harvey?'

'Yes, ma'am,' Harvey said, sounding calm and reassuring after the woman's babble. 'I be Harvey.'

With an effort the woman pulled herself together. 'I'm Mrs Bennings. From Foster Care Services?' She attempted a smile. 'And you two? Why, you must be James and Sarah! All the way from England. My goodness! Well, um ... welcome! Your foster mother, Mrs Slater, she couldn't get into town after

53

all so we'll just jump in my car right now and I'll drive you out there.'

She turned to Harvey, 'Thank you,' she said. Then, 'Children, thank Harvey for taking such good care of you. That's it. Shake hands. And now say goodbye. Sarah, let go of Harvey's hand... Let go this minute! Harvey has to go back to work now. I said, Let go!'

I couldn't see anything through my tears, couldn't talk over the lump in my throat. All I could do was cling fast to Harvey's warm and friendly hand, feeling with an odd certainty that nothing good could possibly lie ahead.

Harvey leaned down to my level. 'I gots to go now, honey,' he said in his kindly way. 'But don't fret. War's gonna be over any day now. Might could be I'll get to take care of you on your way back home.' Disentangling his hand he gave my shoulder a squeeze and hurried away.

James, it turned out, had very little memory of our journey to our new home in Mrs Bennings' car. But I did. I remembered that she didn't pause for breath once as she directed a porter to load our suitcases in the trunk, ushered us into the back seat, climbed into the driver's seat herself, and we set off on what soon began to feel like the length of our journey across the Atlantic.

'You're very lucky little things, yes, sir!' she

exclaimed repeatedly. 'Just think! A few days ago I was at my wits' end trying to figure out what to do with you. Just going crazy knowing I had to find you a place to live. And look at you now! On your way to a real home at last. A fine Catholic home in the country, if you please. Just think about that!

'I wish I could have grown up on a farm in the country,' she went on with a sigh. 'A real farm with cows and pigs and chickens and ducks and fresh vegetables straight from the yard to make me grow up big and strong, Yes, sir!'

Why did she keep saying, 'Yes, sir,' the way she did, I wondered? It made me feel that if I turned quickly I might catch sight of an otherwise invisible man who needed constant reassurance.

'There's hundreds – maybe make that thousands – of kids right here in the United States who'd trade their back teeth to change places with you two, yes, sir!' Mrs Bennings rattled on. 'Growing up in a city is a terrible thing nowadays. Too crowded! Too hot! Too cold! Ask me and I'll tell you because I know. I live in one.'

I could see parts of her face in the rear-view mirror as she spoke. Mostly I saw her mouth and sometimes her eyes when she tilted her head to glance in the mirror to see if she was being listened to.

'I'll tell you what,' the mouth confided. 'If

55

I had more wonderful people like the Slaters my job would be a whole lot easier, yes, sir! Why, I wouldn't have a care in the world. Not a-one. Did you know Mrs Slater raised four fine kids of her own?'

Her eyes took the place of her mouth in the mirror and they were looking straight at me. I knew I was expected to answer but the lump in my throat had once again grown too big to swallow. I shook my head instead.

Mrs Bennings frowned. Oh, dear, a shaking head was not what she wanted. I didn't know what to do next so I gave up and looked out the window.

James, white-faced and blank-eyed, had been staring out of his window since we got in the stuffy car. He wasn't listening to Mrs Bennings at all. I doubted he even knew she was talking.

Mrs Bennings' mouth-in-the-mirror asked, 'What do you think Mrs Slater's own fine kids are doing right now? Take a guess.'

I tried to think what Mrs Slater's fine kids could be doing but really, how could I when the stupid woman had not told me if they were boys or girls or even how old they were?

'All four of them are in the armed services, that's what!' Mrs Bennings said, accompanying her words with a toss of her head as though being in the armed services was a very important place to be. Was it? In England everybody was in the armed services unless they were too old like my father. I tried to smile at the eyes in the mirror.

Mrs Bennings nodded, pleased I was at least paying attention. 'I bet you didn't even know we had armed services over here being we don't have a war going on, huh?

'And does Mrs Slater sit back now and take it easy? No, sir! Now she takes in foster kids. She's already taken in some of my worst cases and now she's helping your country out taking in you refugee kids. She's a fine upstanding American, wouldn't you say?'

She half turned in her seat, looking at me, nodding her head, wanting me to agree with her, but I wasn't quite sure what an up-standing woman was.

Mrs Bennings turned back to face the road and I saw the back of her neck staining red. 'In America,' she hissed, 'we expect children to speak when they are spoken to.'

She nodded to herself and straightened in her seat. 'Let's understand right here, right now, how important it is you two realize just how lucky you are. We've got needy kids right here in the United States you know, and you don't see us shipping them off over-seas. So I expect you both to smile. Are you smiling? That's better.

'Now, where was I? The other kids... Let me see, there's Danny and Cathy and they're brother and sister. Danny must be seven now so that makes Cathy, eight. Then there's

Andy and he's six so his little sister, uh ...
Sally I think her name is, must be going on
five. So! Won't that be fun? All of them right
around your ages.'

James made a small sound aimed at the
back of Mrs Bennings' head as though there
was something he would like to know and I
held my breath, hoping it would be something a grown-up would ask – something
that would put to rest my worries about the
foster parents ahead.

Mrs Bennings had heard the sound and
was leaning forward, her face close to the
mirror, eyes expectant, as though her interest alone could coax words from him.
'Yes?' she encouraged. 'Yes?'

James started slowly. 'I was wondering...
Well ... do you know if any of the children –
I mean the kids – you were telling us about
... do you know if any of them have bicycles?
The two-wheel kind, I mean.'

Mrs Bennings' eyes went round in amazement and the car swerved. 'A bicycle!' she
gasped. 'German bombers blowing England
right off the map and him darn near homeless and all he's got going on in his head is
two-wheel bicycles!'

She started talking to the windshield then,
asking it, 'Did you hear that? Don't that just
beat all? I find him a fine home in the country, a Catholic home in the country, mind,
with homegrown food and healthy fresh air

and kids his own age and all he's got going on in his head are two-wheel bicycles!'

Her eyes in the mirror sought James. 'I don't know,' she shrugged. 'You couldn't ride one even if they all have two-wheel bicycles. In America a farm means fields and woods and barns and chickens and cows and dirt roads and no sidewalks. There's no place out there to ride a bicycle!' She went on shaking her head and frowning and making little clucking noises but at least she stopped talking and that was one thing less to think about when there was already so much else to sort through: cows and chickens and pigs, the amazing Mrs Slater, the other kids we were going to love because they were right around our age.

Mrs Bennings sighed and rolled her eyes. 'We'll be there any minute now. Just over the next hill if I'm not mistaken. It's just a dirt road turn-off you see, and with no rain in weeks and all the dust, it will be easy to miss so you'll have to help me out.'

It was my turn to roll my eyes then, thinking, there she goes again, expecting us to know things, help her, when we don't even know where we are.

But then I had a sudden memory of leaving the ship and Alf, then the train and dear old Harvey and now, as ridiculous as this Mrs Bennings woman was, I knew I'd rather go on riding in the back seat of her car till the war was over than face the foster parents ahead.

There came a sudden screech of brakes, a scream from Mrs Bennings, and we were going in reverse. James and I had both tumbled to the floor but Mrs Bennings hadn't noticed. She was too busy talking. 'Isn't this exciting? I bet Mrs Slater is counting the minutes. I told her about twelve so we're only a little over an hour late. Wait till you taste her cooking. Yum! Yum! Everything home grown and homemade. You two are most definitely the luckiest little kids in this whole entire world.'

We, the lucky little kids, crawled back in our seats and looked out the windows. We were driving through thick woods and thick dust and it was very bumpy.

'My, but it's dry out here, isn't it?' Mrs Bennings exclaimed. 'I told you they haven't had rain in weeks. Keep looking up ahead now and you'll soon see the house. I do believe the trees are thinning... Yes! There! Look! Your wonderful, wonderful new home.'

She brought the car to a stop in front of split-rail fencing nailed between several trees. There was no gate in the fence and I wondered how people were meant to get in and out.

Through the slowly settling dust we could make out a tall, narrow, brown-shingled house at the end of a dried-up lawn. A porch ran across the front of the house and down one side. From the other side a narrow, elevated cement path streaked towards the fence we were in front of where it stopped abruptly, as though taken aback by the massive trees behind us.

'Is this the country?' I asked, thinking if it was, I couldn't understand why everyone made such a fuss.

In the front seat, Mrs Bennings was busy smacking her nose with a powder puff. She paused long enough to say, 'Sarah, if this isn't the country, then I'd just like for you to tell me what is.'

'In England,' I said, 'this would be called woods.'

'What you need to get through your head, Miss Sarah, is that England isn't your home anymore, is it?'

I would have liked to tell her that if anyone had bothered to ask me, it would be, but Mrs Bennings was already talking again. 'Come along now, time to get your suitcases out of the trunk. I'd think you'd be glad to get out and stretch your legs. I know I sure am.'

I took my case reluctantly, as though by accepting it I was accepting my situation when, in reality, I longed to drop it, kick it, and say, 'Never mind. I shan't be staying,' but just then James nudged me and, with a sideways glance, indicated a short, dumpy woman walking towards us along the cement path from the direction of the house, one hand up shading her eyes the better to see us. We both knew it could only be the amazing Mrs Slater.

My heart lurched and we both looked away quickly knowing instantly that, just as Mummy had been quite wrong in extolling the charms of Escort and the ship, she had been equally wrong about this foster mother. For even from a distance we could see this was not the dear, sweet, kind person that she had so cheerfully envisioned for us.

Mrs Slater's appearance alone told us she was quite the opposite. She wore a big, unfriendly frown on her forehead, ugly wire-rimmed glasses on her nose, and a faded, shapeless, navy and white print dress. Her stockings were rolled down to mid-calf and a pair of unlaced men's shoes adorned her feet. Her wispy, greying hair was twisted into a bun on the back of her head.

A wave of fear surged through us both and delayed car sickness flooded me, making my legs feel weak and shaky. I longed for someone familiar to cling to: Mummy... Alf... Harvey... Oh, just anyone.

I sagged against the car and everything blurred. My car-sickness had caught up with me in earnest and I started to vomit. It went everywhere.

'Oh, my God!' Mrs Bennings shrieked. 'She's ruined my shoes. James! James, look away! Get a-hold of yourself, boy! Don't you dare start in, too!'

Stepping out of her shoes she stumbled towards Mrs Slater, her voice changing to a moan. 'Agnes! Oh, Agnes, you aren't going to believe these two. All this way and hardly a word out of either one of them and now this! At least she saved it till she got out of the car. Couldn't have taken driving all the way back to town with that stink in the back seat.'

Taking me by the elbow, Mrs Bennings pulled me away from the car, lined James up beside me and, stepping back, arms stretched wide, head tilted to one side like the statue of the angel in our English church, bowed. 'Agnes, dear, meet your new additions, James and Sarah.'

Agnes stepped down from the cement path, losing several of her scant inches in the process, and looking dumpier than ever. By bending at the waist and inserting her bulk through the rails of the fence, she demonstrated one possible procedure for entering and exiting her property.

Standing before us, lips smiling but eyes suspicious in her sweat-beaded face, she said, 'I want you should call me Mother.' Following that with a sniff and navigating the fence in the same manner as before but going in the opposite direction, she added, 'You're late. We've been waitin' on you. Come on up the house now, meet the other kids.'

FOUR

Following Agnes' demonstration, Mrs Bennings navigated the fence in the same manner but, in what he now remembers as a feeble attempt at independence, James chose to climb over it. Doubtless seeking my own independence and seeing that the fence only extended to three trees, I simply walked around the end one and fell into step behind James on the narrow cement path on its other side.

With Agnes leading the way, we walked past the front porch and along the side of the house to the last door on our right, which opened into the kitchen.

'Get your noses out them picture books, kids,' Agnes ordered, opening the squealing screen door.

Four skinny, dusty-looking, barefoot little kids, all dressed alike in tattered overalls, their sex apparent only by the shaved heads of the boys, were sitting on a bench against one wall. Setting aside their unopened books they stared up at us.

Pointing to each in turn and barking out their names as her finger moved along the line, Agnes addressed them as though they were army recruits, 'Danny, Cathy, Sally, Andy, these two new ones is called, uh...'

'James and Sarah,' coached Mrs Bennings.

'Yeah,' Agnes said. 'That's right. James and Sarah.' Turning to Mrs Bennings, she said, 'Go ahead and leave them suitcases right there in my office for now,' she nodded towards a small adjoining room, 'and come dig in. Like I said, you're late.'

'Oh, Agnes...' Mrs Bennings faltered, setting down the suitcases as directed and massaging her fingers, '...first I think a trip to the uh ... toilet for all of us. Such a long drive... Over two hours...'

From the scowl on her face it was clear Agnes wasn't happy with that idea. 'I still ain't got runnin' water,' she complained. 'But,' she brightened, 'I got me a new cement walkway makes it easier gettin' out there now. Cathy, take and show 'em.'

Cathy, who was smaller than me and very pretty with the kind of long, golden braids I had always dreamed of, led Mrs Bennings, James and me, again in single file, outside to a little shed next to a chicken run where dozens of chickens were crowded into a small patch of shade. Cathy stopped and pointed to the door of the little shed.

Mrs Bennings stepped forward and pushed it open and I could see what looked like a wooden bench with two side-by-side holes cut in it. Such awful smells came through the open door I felt sick all over again.

'Look, Sarah,' Mrs Bennings chirped, 'it's an old timey two-seater so we can go together. James, you'll have to wait.'

With a hasty shake of my head, I declined the invitation and Mrs Bennings braved the stench alone. The Cathy girl looked at James, 'If you just need to pee, you can go upside the wall like Danny and Andy does if you want,' she suggested.

We both stared at her. Did she mean he should unbutton his trousers and just aim for the side of the shed? When James didn't move, Cathy rolled her eyes. 'Go round back then if you don't want me lookin',' she glowered. 'Je-sus!'

James hesitated and then disappeared around the back of the shed but I knew he couldn't have done anything because he wasn't gone long enough to even unbutton his trousers, never mind button them back up.

Back in the kitchen, Mrs Bennings walked around the table clapping her hands and screeching about all the wonderful, wonderful, home-grown, home-cooked food and suddenly both James and I were glad she did talk so much. It kept Agnes from asking us about the bombs and the ration books in England. And from telling us how lucky we were to be there, safe at last, in her ghastly house.

'Sit! Eat!' Agnes commanded.

Nobody had to tell the four resident kids to eat. From the moment they sat down they didn't stop and really, I thought they were quite disgusting. I couldn't really tell what the little Sally girl sitting next to me looked like because her straight, brown hair was falling over her face, but I could see her mouth in profile through that curtain of hair and she had so much food in it the poor little thing couldn't close it.

Feeling just a bit sorry for her, I said as quietly as I could, 'It's rude to chew with your mouth open, you know.'

Agnes gasped, 'What'd she just say?'

Mrs Bennings giggled a feeble little giggle and said, 'I think you should leave table manners to Mother Slater, Sarah.'

Knowing perfectly well I shouldn't say another word and knowing James' eyes across the table were begging me not to, I nevertheless felt so disgusted and upset with the events of the whole horrible day culminating in this depressingly, awful place with ugly, fat Agnes for a foster mother, I thought, What's the use her being at the table if she isn't going to teach these dirty little kids some manners? Turning to Agnes, I said, 'Don't you think you should tell that boy sitting next to you to take his elbows off the table?'

'That's enough, Sarah,' Mrs Bennings snapped.

'Jesus Christ!' Agnes gasped, 'Knew I should've waited and gotten me reg'lar American kids!'

After filling and emptying her plate twice over, Mrs Bennings began hinting that she must soon leave. She stood up and looked around the table as though to assure herself that everyone was paying attention.

'I'm going straight back to town now,' she announced, 'write up my report. Try and get a letter in the mail to these kids' parents let them know they are finally in the kind of home they'd been praying for: a fine, decent, Catholic home in the country with kids their own age.'

Continuing as if James and I weren't in the room, she said, 'I'm expecting to hear great things about James and Sarah from Mother Slater so they'd better be good and do as they're told.'

Turning to Agnes, she added, 'No need for you to get up, dear. I'll see myself out. Goodness knows I know the way by now!'

Her hand on the screen-door handle, she paused. 'Thank you, Agnes,' she cooed. 'Thank you more than I can say. Not only are you giving these kids a fine home but you saved my neck!'

She was almost through the door when she evidently remembered something important and turned back gasping. 'Agnes! I nearly forgot to ask. Your husband ... um ... Walter, isn't it? He is ... I mean ... he is out of the house now, right?'

'Yeah. He's out.' Agnes spluttered over a mouthful of food. 'Fixed up that old cabin back in the woods for hisself and the boys and don't come in no more but to eat.'

Mrs Bennings smiled, waved her hand and said, 'I knew we could count on you.' Blowing a farewell kiss she was gone.

Head to one side, Agnes sat motionless as Mrs Bennings went on her merry way. The kids sat motionless, too, staring down at their empty plates. Agnes frowned when she saw me studying her, taking in her sweaty face and the big hole under the arm of her ugly dress, so I looked away but I knew something. I knew she didn't like me. Didn't, in fact, like kids at all.

With Mrs Bennings gone, Agnes pushed back from the table. 'You boys take the Limey over to the cabin, get him in overalls and show him what haulin's all about,' she said. 'Cathy, you and Sally get this kitchen cleaned up and no dawdlin', hear? I want you both out haulin', too, else how'm I sup-posed to feed you come winter with not a drop of rain in three weeks?'

James followed the boys outside. Cathy and the Sally girl started carrying the dirty dishes from the table to the sink and Agnes strode into the little room next to the kitchen, the one she called her office. I was left sitting at the table alone.

Squinting at the faded oilcloth table cover trying to make out what the original pattern might have been, I thought how perfectly ridiculous it was to call an ordinary room with only a rocking chair and a telephone in it an office. Having been in my father's office more than once I knew perfectly well it didn't qualify as one at all. Besides, everybody knew women didn't have offices. Only men.

Agnes' voice interrupted my thoughts and I realized she wasn't in her office after all. She was standing in the doorway between the two rooms with a big frown on her face looking down on me.

'I said, is that what-all you do in England?' she snarled. 'Set, when there's work waitin' to get done? That ain't how we do things around here.'

I was too shocked to answer. All I could think to do was stand up and in doing so I brought the table cover up with me. I tried to smooth it back down.

'Cathy, give her the dish towel, let her finish up while you sweep,' Agnes ordered. She stopped to rub her forehead and while she did, the girls stood the way the soldiers stand outside Buckingham Palace – at attention.

Only when Agnes turned away and we heard what turned out to be the rocking chair rumbling on the wood floor next door in the office, did they start to move again.

There was a lot of food left on the table and while they were putting it away Cathy and Sally ate the scraps Mrs Bennings had left on the side of her plate. Cathy took a bite off a chicken leg and Sally picked up half a bread roll – ugh, it had lipstick all over it – and stuffed it in one of the pockets of her overalls.

They took food from the serving dishes, too, sliding potato salad and sliced tomatoes and beets up the sides of the bowls with their fingers and, heads turned away from the direction of the office making it clear they weren't supposed to be taking it, stuffing it in their mouths.

I started to ask Cathy where I should put the dishes I dried but stopped because, looking ferocious, she was shaking her head at me and pointing to the office.

'Shut up,' her lips mouthed.

I made an ugly face at her. How was I supposed to know where to put stuff if I wasn't allowed to ask? Cathy grabbed me by the elbow, pointed this way, then the other, and I followed her pointing finger as best I could until all the dishes were put away and the kitchen swept. She then motioned me to follow her and Sally outside.

Agnes saw us shuffling past the office doorway and stopped her rocking to call out to me, 'Get them shoes off, girl. We don't waste good shoe leather around here in summertime. Cathy, run up get her a pair of your overalls. Want you all out haulin'. Sally, reach outside give that bell a ring. You know well's I do it's time for them boys to start in milkin'. How come I have to think of everythin'?'

Sitting on the floor, I took my shoes and socks off as Cathy came thudding down the stairs with a pair of limp overalls in her hand. 'Here,' she said, thrusting them at me, 'put 'em on.'

I looked around, 'Where?' I asked.

'Right here.'

'Here? I can't. It's rude to take your clothes off in front of other people.'

The rocking chair stopped rocking and Agnes again filled the doorframe. My dress came off. My slip. My little gold bangle bracelet. My St Christopher medal. Interestingly, I was never to see those last two items ever again.

Barefoot, wearing Cathy's overalls, and fighting back tears, I followed the girls outside.

'Haulin'' was all about carrying empty buckets over a hill in the woods and down the other side to a well. The well didn't have a pretty little brick wall around it surrounded by flowers like the ones in picture books. This well was just a hole in the ground with a couple of flat stones either side of it.

To get the water out you hooked a bucket to a rope and then wound a handle attached to a pole so the bucket went deep in the hole. I leaned over the edge to see where the water was but it was so far down all I could see was a far-away kind of shine that made me dizzy.

When you got the rope unwound as far as it would go you gave it a jiggle so the bucket at the end of it would tip over and fill up and then you wound the handle back the other way. Bringing it back up was much harder than lowering it and it took two of us, really straining, to bring it up and lift it out of the well. When our three buckets were full we carried them back up the hill with Cathy carrying not only her own bucket but one side of Sally's as well. Agnes was waiting for us at the edge of a huge vegetable field, one foot tapping with impatience.

'Full buckets,' she roared as we arrived beside her. 'These is half empty, Godammit. It's my vegetables need water, not your feet. Here, take'n pour one of 'em on these here beans. You must've skimped 'em yesterday. Damn things is near dead. You want to eat come winter?'

We poured where Agnes pointed and then ran back down to the well and I wondered why we couldn't just walk. After a few more trips I asked Cathy how many more buckets we were going to have to haul, '...because,' I said, 'I'm tired of running behind you and Agnes shouting at us when we get back and my feet are getting all cut and bruised from the stones on the path and the inside of my hands are getting blisters. Look. Besides, I don't want to haul anymore.'

'More'n you can count,' Cathy answered. 'Soon's we get done with the vegetables we got to haul two to the hogs and two to the cows and one to the chickens and three for inside the house.'

To pay Cathy back for saying I couldn't count, I sat down with my back to her in a patch of shade next to the well.

'You better move your backside 'less you want old Agnes down here movin' it for you,' Cathy warned.

'I'm tired. I'm resting,' I said, putting my head down on my knees to show how very tired I was.

'Yeah?' Cathy marvelled. 'Well, guess what? You ain't here to rest. You're here to work. Want to know somethin' else? She's expectin' you and that brother of yours to work harder'n us on account of you're bigger'n us.'

She looked at me sideways. 'Not but that either one of you is near big enough, you ask me. Not near as big as Annie and Billy was and that's what she'd been countin' on.'

More than anything else just then I would have liked to scream and shout and hit that hateful little girl. And cry. But I wouldn't. What, and have her call me a crybaby? No, indeed I would not. Never, never, never.

But then ... where was that terrible howling noise coming from? Not Cathy or Sally, both staring at me with round, startled eyes.

It was me!

All the time I'd been hauling I kept thinking I'd look up and see my mother, or perhaps Alf, coming towards me saying, 'There you are! I told you the war would be over soon, didn't I? Come on, it's time to go home now.'

But no matter how often I looked up – quickly, so I'd see them before they saw me – they never came. And that's when I began to suspect they probably never would.

'You keep up that racket and she'll give you something to bawl about, I tell you what,' Cathy growled. 'She'll beat you till the shit comes out of you, is what she'll do.'

She squatted down beside me and started talking like a tired old lady who knows everything. 'I knew it'd go like this,' she sighed. 'Did when Sally and Andy first come. Takin' up my good time with their cryin'... Gettin' cuts and blisters and sores... Wantin' to talk and ask dumb questions the live long day like as if I'm God and know everythin'.'

She sighed again. 'It's gonna go worse with you two,' she went on, 'on account of she's worse. Every day a little bit worse. Been like that ever since Annie and Billy got took away.'

I stopped crying to ask who Annie and Billy were but Cathy didn't answer and I suddenly saw why. It was because the whole time she'd been squatting beside me talking she'd been peeing and watching it trickle down the slight incline on which we perched.

Standing, Cathy hitched the straps of her overalls back over her shoulders and told me I ought to go, too. She said, 'Agnes gets goin' later on she won't let you, and then she'll get to beat you up for makin' a puddle.'

'I haven't made a puddle since I was a baby,' I said with a toss of my head. 'And it's rude to pull your pants down so other people can see your bottom.'

And then I started crying even harder than before and I was just so disappointed in myself. But every time Cathy said something there was more and more to be frightened about. Especially the bit about Agnes getting worse every day. How bad could worse get?

Cathy turned away from me. 'Come on, Sally,' she called. 'Let's just leave her cry. We need to get these buckets up to them damn vegetables 'fore she comes wantin' to know where we're at.'

I stopped crying the instant they left because I realized I was alone and what if Agnes did come looking for me and beat the shit out of me – could that really happen? –

like Cathy said she would.

I ran to catch up with them even though my feet hurt even worse than before, but I thought I'd feel safer being with them than by myself. When I got to where I could see them up ahead, I changed my mind again and decided to wait but Cathy had seen me and called out that Agnes had gone in to fix supper and we needed to get a move on. Getting a move on meant hauling eight more buckets from the well and distributing them, then putting the buckets away in the barn.

In the barn two cows were tied up and James was sitting on a little stool trying to get milk out of one of them. Danny and Andy were leaning against the wall laughing so hard they were doubled over but James wasn't. He was frowning and biting his lip not to cry.

Cathy was furious. 'You mean all this time you two been fallin' around laughin' when you know good and well she'll be after you with the pitchfork that milk don't get up to the house right quick? Jesus! Get out the way, James, let Danny finish up.'

Danny and James changed places and the milk started gushing out of that cow as though he had turned on a tap. I was fascinated and asked if I could have a turn but Cathy wouldn't let me. 'Milkin' ain't for fun,' she glowered, 'It's work. Like everythin' else around here.'

She turned on Danny again, 'What you think you was doin' teachin' him on Suzy anyways when everyone knows she's the meanest damn cow in the county? Lucky for you she didn't take and butt him clean out the barn and break both his arms like she done Billy that one time.'

'Shut up and stop bein' so damn bossy,' Danny told her. 'You sound worse'n Agnes and it wasn't my fault. I started him on ole Clara but he never did get the hang of it so I told Andy to finish up with her while I tried teachin' him on Suzy. How was I s'posed to know he'd be such a dumb jerk, huh?'

'It's you the jerk!' Cathy fumed.

Danny bunched up his fist to hit her but just then a bell started clanging and he relaxed his fist.

'Bell means we got to go in to supper,' Cathy said.

'I'm not hungry,' I sniffled. 'Please tell her ... Agnes ... I'd rather just stay outside for now, thank you.'

'Tell her that and you're liable to stay out all night,' Cathy snorted. 'Shut up in the barn here with crazy Suzy and ole Clara.'

I wasn't sure what liable meant but I thought I'd better go in with the others.

At the back of the house stood a rickety wooden stand with a basin of water on it – dirty brown water with bits of leaves and

78

grass floating on its surface. The kids dipped their fingertips in it, rubbed at their eyes, then dried their fingers by rubbing them, fronts and backs, on their overall legs. James and I did the same.

An old man with a bald head and glasses was sitting hunched over a newspaper at the table in the kitchen when we walked in. Agnes didn't introduce us but I was pretty sure it was Mr Slater. I was glad to see he didn't look the least little bit like my father.

The food set out for supper wasn't at all like the huge spread of homegrown, home-made food that had sent Mrs Bennings into such raptures earlier.

For supper there was just a soup bowl in front of each chair and beside it a slice of bread and half a glass of milk. In each bowl floated a chicken's foot, its talons curled in on themselves. What were we supposed to do with them?

Ignoring the steam curling up from their bowls, the other kids plunged their fingers into the hot soup, pulled out the feet and started gnawing them. James copied them but had to stop almost at once to pull fragments of bone from between his teeth. I thought I'd just roll my bread into little balls and eat those and then ask for a second helping of pudding.

When all the bowls but mine were empty, Agnes reached across the table, took it and handed it to Cathy. 'Feed it to the hogs,' she said.

Next to the sink stood a bucket where we'd poured the dirty, greasy dishwater and various inedible food scraps after lunch. Cathy added my soup to the mix. Poor hogs, I thought, feeling sorry for them while wondering if 'hogs' was American for pigs.

There was no pudding and you didn't have to wait to be excused from the table in that house. As soon as you finished eating you just got up and left. That first night James was a bit uncertain as to the procedure and waited to follow Andy. They were sidling behind the man's chair when he reached up and touched James' elbow.

'How's the war goin', son?' he asked.

James blinked. He didn't know how the war was going.

'You know, the one you got goin' on over in England,' the man persisted.

'Godammit it, Walter,' Agnes growled. 'He ain't here to stand around gabbin' about no war. What's he know anyways? Let him finish his work and get on over to the cabin.'

We dispersed, much as we had after lunch, with the boys and Mr Slater going to the cabin – a small square wooden building we had passed many times in the woods while hauling water – Agnes to her rocker in the office, and the girls to the sink. When the last dish was put away and the floor swept, we lined up in front of her.

'Get your backsides on up to bed,' she said. 'Cathy, you and what's-her-name take them suitcases up with you. Sally bring in the pot.'

Sally disappeared outside and came back carrying a white enamel bucket nearly as big as herself. Clanking behind Cathy and me on the stairs with it, she yelped as at each step the bucket swiped her shins.

At the top of the stairs we walked straight ahead into a room that had a double bed pushed against one wall and a single bed against another. In a corner was a kind of alcove and inside that stood another little bed. The wood floors were bare and I winced walking across them on my battered feet. There were no pictures on the wall or curtains at the window of that room.

There was another door at the top of the stairs, which was closed. The space between the two doors was where Sally put the bucket.

Just as Agnes had demonstrated earlier how to manoeuvre her fence, she now demonstrated the use of the bucket. My exhausted, tear-swollen eyes widened as I watched her hoist up the skirt of her dress, squat over it and, with a sigh of satisfaction, empty her bladder. The noise was amazing, louder than twin taps filling a deep bathtub.

In the bedroom, Agnes lifted the suitcases

81

onto the big bed, opened them, and gasped with anger.

'Why, there ain't nothin' worth two dimes in here!' she spluttered. 'Just a bunch of wore out summer stuff. Looks like Miss England's gonna freeze come winter, don't it? Don't see no boots. No leggin's. No coats. No gloves. No damn all.'

She set the suitcases on the floor with a thump of disgust and began pulling her dress over her head, shocking me all over again. This time at the sight of a naked adult, the first I'd ever seen. Did everyone have hair there, I wondered? How disgusting. It was only then that I realized something that had escaped me when she was using the bucket: Agnes wasn't wearing any underwear! Not even knickers!

'You wet the bed, girl?' she asked me, pulling a rag of a nightgown over her head.

Before I could think of a polite way to remind her that I was nearly six, she grabbed me by the shoulders and began to shake me. 'Around here we answer when we're asked a question,' she panted. 'And it's "Yes, ma'am" or "No, ma'am" to me. And it's "Yes, sir" and "No, sir" to him. You got that?'

I started to nod my head again but remembered just in time and gasped, 'Yes, ma'am.'

'That's more like it,' she glowered and, pulling back the sheet of the big bed, motioned me to get in. 'You're sleepin' with me,' she said. 'Slide on over to the wall. Any thrashin' around and you're on the floor. Cathy, turn out that light and start in prayin'.'

I had to sleep with her? In the same bed? But ... I couldn't. I wouldn't! I'd never slept in the same bed with anyone – except occasionally Mummy when I was sick – in my whole life.

'I ... I haven't brushed my teeth yet,' I quavered. 'And ... I have to find my nightie. Have you seen it?'

Agnes picked me up, tossed me on the bed, and saying, 'We don't got no bathroom nor time for brushing teeth around here,' pulled off my overalls and tossed them on the floor. The light went out.

While I was busy making sure I was as close to the wall as I could get, Cathy and Sally began droning the rosary. Agnes' foot crossed the bed and kicked me. 'Pray,' she growled. 'I said you'd get religion.'

It wasn't easy getting the whole rosary past the lump in my throat, but at least it was dark and I didn't have to worry about any of them seeing my tears.

FIVE

As we continued delving ever deeper into our pasts, a diversion that was beginning to consume us almost to the exclusion of our own families, James and I found ourselves reverting to the way we talked back then and the vocabulary we used, or rather, I should say, that Agnes used, in those far-off days.

For example, her term for walking was, lollygaggin' – something she would not put up with.

'Too much work around here for you-all to be lollygaggin' along like you got all day,' she'd roar. 'Move it! Get haulin'! Feed them hogs! Pull them weeds! Churn that butter! Bring in them cows! Feed them hens! Collect them eggs! Clean up this room! Hang out that wash! Iron up his shirts! Mop that floor!'

The only nice thing that ever happened, the only time we could walk instead of run, was when our turn came around to go to the store, and even then we ran until we were out of sight of the house. A 'turn' came around every six days unless we did something to make Agnes angry – mad – in which case someone else got it and we had to wait another long six days. Agnes had to watch herself there, though, not to be mad at all of us at once thereby leaving her with nobody to send. It happened once. She compromised by sending Sally, saying the kid was so dumb she didn't know the difference between a treat and a punishment and in this instance she was being punished.

We didn't go to the store every day to buy things. 'Are you nuts?' Cathy exclaimed when I asked why we hardly ever did. 'Agnes only buys stuff she can't figure how to grow or make her own self. Stuff like coffee, sugar, flour, yeast.

'Why she sends us every day,' she elaborated, 'is on account of the store ain't just a store, see. It's a Post Office as well and we need to pick up her mail. Mail she 'spects from her kids every day but don't hardly never get.'

James and I hadn't been living with Agnes a week when we learned that receiving a letter from England was one of the worst things that could happen to us. It made Agnes go what Cathy called 'crazy-mad', and we both lost our turns to go to the store the following week.

Cathy explained why. 'You-all gettin' mail when she don't is bad enough on account of it makes her out a liar, bein' she's all the time sayin' that war you got goin' on over there is how come her mail don't get through. But James takin' and openin' and readin' his like he done was what got him that black eye. That was just plain dumb.'

'But Mummy addressed it to him,' I protested.

Cathy shrugged. 'Don't mean he gets to open it,' she growled.

'If any letters come from England when it's my turn to go to the store I shan't tell Agnes about them,' I said. 'I'll just hide them until James can read them to me and then I'll tear them up in little pieces and throw them away and she'll never know.'

Cathy said she would, too, know. She said, 'That day James took and opened his I heard her on the telephone tellin' Bill – Bill being the man who owned the store – that any time mail comes in from England he was to give her a call and let her know about it.'

I thought about that a moment before saying, 'I don't care who she told what because just as soon as I can get some money for a stamp I'm going to write and tell my parents what a wicked, beastly woman Agnes is and they'll write to someone, Mrs Roosevelt probably, and we'll get taken someplace else.'

Cathy said we wouldn't neither. She said, 'When Agnes got done tellin' Bill about the mail comin' in from England, she told him no mail was to go out neither. Not 'less it had her handwritin' on the outside.'

'You're just making that up because you and Danny don't get any mail from anyone,'

I glowered. 'Not ever.'

'You're dumber even than I thought,' Cathy sighed, in a pitying kind of way. 'How're me and Danny supposed to get mail bein' we're orphans?'

'If you were nice orphans I expect you would,' I said. 'And anyway, who cares? If I can't send a letter I'll think of some other way to get away from this beastly, horrible place because no matter what, I'm not staying and neither is James.'

'Don't much matter what you figure to do,' Cathy said over a yawn, 'You're way too little for it to count.'

Some days I hated her more than others, that Cathy.

To get to the store, you followed the path to the well, then kept on going. After the well, I noticed that the path seemed wider and friendlier with fewer rocks, some nice cool patches of moss to step on and, depending on the season, pretty clumps of wild flowers.

The path ended at the back of the store and there you had to be extra careful where you walked in your bare feet. There were broken bottles, mouldering newspapers, an ancient bed spring, rusty cans, and old tyres everywhere. There was even a nasty, pee-stained mattress with a big black hole burned in the middle of it, which none of us could ever pass without wondering if anyone had been on it when the fire started and got burned alive.

The first time I went to the store, Cathy went with me to show me the way and we ran all the way there and back even though Cathy knew perfectly well that Agnes never, ever went past the well.

'Why do you run the whole way when you don't have to?' I once asked her. 'Agnes can't see you once you get over the hill.'

'Bein' away from Agnes to where I can't watch her face and try'n figure what's comin' next scares me worse than bein' up close and gettin' beat up,' Cathy said. 'I run so's I can get back'n keep a eye on her.'

'I don't see what good keeping an eye on her does because you do, too, know what's coming next,' I reasoned. 'She's going to shout – yell – at you and beat the shit out of you is what's coming next.'

When you got around to the front of the store you saw it was on a paved road, not a dirt one, and that there was a row of little houses opposite where you could see people out in their gardens – yards – acting normal. Normal being our definition of the way people acted who knew nothing about a wicked, fat old woman called Agnes living back in the woods who was cruel and beat up little kids. Some days you could even hear radio music coming from those houses.

The first time I saw all that activity I

stopped in my tracks and stared I was so surprised.

'What?' Cathy asked, exasperated.

'When Mrs Bennings brought us out here we didn't pass any houses or people for miles and miles and I thought nobody lived out here but us.'

Cathy had a way of rolling her eyes when she thought she was the only person in the world who knew anything. She rolled them then.

''Course there's people,' she glowered. 'There's people everywhere. Used to be we even had comp'ny at the house oncc in a while like Agnes' sister, Martha, and her husband and such.'

I was going to ask why they didn't come anymore but just then a pretty young mother came around the side of one of the houses with two dear little girls and they were all giggling.

Sighing with envy, I said, 'I do wish we'd been sent over there to live with that sweet, pretty lady instead of nasty, fat old Agnes.'

Cathy looked the little group over, her eyes narrowing as though she was studying some disgusting species of bug. 'Not me,' she said. 'I got me a way sweeter, prettier Mommy than her picked out and we live in a way prettier house.'

'If you were as clever as you think you are,' I told her, narrowing my own eyes, 'you

89

would have realized – figured out – by now that kids like us aren't allowed to pick who we want to live with. We have to go where we're sent. Anyway, where is she, this sweet, pretty, perfect mother you have picked out?'

'Next time you go poop, take a look in that old Sears catalogue hangin' on the nail, page eighty-nine, and you'll see her,' Cathy said, looking happy for once. 'She's wearin' a real pretty dress and high-heeled shoes and she's fixin' pancakes at an electric stove, and...' she paused to be sure she had my full attention, 'our kitchen's got frilly curtains at the window.

'We all got real pretty mommies picked out in that there catalogue,' she continued after she was sure I had been impressed by the curtains, 'and you better never rip out page eighty-nine to wipe your butt, else look out.'

I felt so sorry for her. I said, 'You can't pick out real live mothers from pictures.'

'Yeah?' Cathy countered. 'Then if pictures don't count, that picture of your mother Agnes took out of your suitcase that time don't count neither.'

'Yes, it does!'

'Then how come you're here, huh?' Cathy taunted. 'Your mother ain't takin' care of you, is she? Heck, she din't even want you in the house.'

'Just you wait and you'll see,' I howled, so

90

mad I felt like crying. 'Any day now the war will be over and Alf from the ship will come and take us home and that frilly lady making pancakes is never going – ain't never gonna – come find you.'

'So what?' Cathy jeered. 'I don't need nobody comin' to find me. All I got to do is grow up and then I can go find her my own self, so shut your big trap!'

The inside of the store was as messy as the outside and we kids loved every inch of it, right down to the way it smelled with its combined odours of tobacco smoke, coffee, smoked hams, beer, chicken feed, pickles and the unwashed smell of Bill himself. A mix so pungent that the kids who hadn't been to the store on any given day could smell it hours later on the one who had.

The first time I went to the store, Cathy told me that if I said yes to everything Bill said and laughed at all his corny jokes, he'd let me pick out a piece of candy from the candy case. For free!

Holy smoke!

On the days it wasn't your turn to go to the store, that candy case was all we could think about, with each of us knowing exactly which piece we were going to choose when our turn came around again.

There was another time I went to the store with Cathy because – on account of – Agnes was canning fruit and needed more sugar than either one of us could carry by ourselves.

Naturally, we ran all the way and when we crashed through the ancient screen door, Bill looked up and said, 'Danged if that don't beat all. We got England in the mail today and Miss England herself runnin' through the door.'

He was waving a letter over his head with Mummy's handwriting on it that I was expected to jump for. It made me wonder which adult I hated most. My mother for writing when her letters got me in trouble and all she ever talked about was how thrilled she and Daddy were that we were living in a lovely home in the country with such wonderful, wonderful people. Or Bill, who wouldn't give me the candy I'd been drooling over and dreaming about for days if I didn't keep jumping up and down like a flea reaching for it.

Just when I'd think I'd got it, he'd laugh and raise his hand still higher, and that's when he saw the big purple lump on my forehead and laughed harder still.

'What happened to you, girl?' he wheezed. 'You fall out the hayloft?'

I kept jumping and reaching for the letter, I had to, while saying, 'No, sir. I didn't fall out the hayloft. Agnes – Mother – got very cross – mad – at me and gave me a spank–

uh ... lickin'. The buckle on the belt is what made that lump.'

Right away Bill stopped laughing and from the corner of my eye I saw that Cathy wasn't looking in the candy case anymore but at me instead, a look of scorn on her face. My legs began to shake wondering what I'd said wrong.

'You standin' there tellin' me you give that good woman trouble to where she's got to whup you?' Bill glowered. 'Shame on you. Her taking in all you no-count brats. Givin' you a fine home.'

Shoving the sugar across the counter, he pointed to the door. 'Get on home now,' he growled, ''fore I tan the hide offa you myself.'

Outside, Cathy shoved me up against the side of the store and, her face right in mine, hissed, 'It's on account of you we din't get no candy!'

She was so cross – mad – her eyes were watering. She shoved me again. 'When you gonna learn to lie, huh? You'd have said, "Yeah, I fell out the hayloft smack dab on top of a pitchfork," he'd have said you was one fine girl and we'd be eatin' our candy.'

'It's wicked to lie,' I hissed back. 'My mother said so and so did the nuns and even our priest.'

'Not when you ain't never got enough to eat, it ain't,' Cathy glowered.

She turned to walk away, paused, turned

back, shoved me against the wall a third time. 'You never picked up your damn mail,' she said, and went back in the store to get it.

She came out waving mail, not just Mummy's letter but another one as well, and her cheek bulging. She puffed her breath in my face. 'Butterscotch!' she smirked. 'Serve you right.'

Agnes saw the mail sticking out of Cathy's overall bib pocket the minute we walked in the door and took the time to look pained. 'Jesus!' she sighed, 'Not another one of them Limey letters. Wisht all I had to do was set writin' letters while other folks minded my kids.'

'There's another one, too, ma'am, look!' Cathy said, waving both pieces.

Agnes snatched the mail, slipped Mummy's in her apron pocket and ripped open the other. Almost at once her face twisted in scorn, 'Do you beat that?' she glowered coming to the end.

I never did know how to answer when Agnes asked, 'Do you beat that?' Beat what?

'Some old biddies from hereabouts, request...' Agnes read out loud, her eyebrows arching, 'the pleasure of my company at a Knittin' Bee! Want me out helpin' the Red Cross knit up stuff for them bomb victims over in England.'

She shook her head in disbelief. 'The nerve of 'em when I'm already doin' more'n my share for the war victims with Limey brats right here in my own house!'

From the way she was looking at me, as though it was all my fault, I thought I'd better say something quickly or get slapped.

'Everybody knitted in England, too,' I said. 'They thought it was patriotic,' I added, trying to make it sound as if they'd all gone mad over there, too.

I got my face slapped anyway. 'Did I ask you?'

Before her hand could come back the other way, I hastily added, 'I hated it!'

But Agnes wasn't listening. She was thinking. 'You can always tell when she's thinking,' Cathy had once explained. 'It's when she rolls her bottom lip between her thumb and fingers.'

Her thinking over, Agnes let go of her lip and said, 'You tellin' me you know knittin'? A little kid your age? Who taught you?'

'My Mummy. We knitted scarves and socks for the soldiers and sailors.'

Agnes' eyebrows went up. 'And did Mummy,' she tried to pronounce the word as I had, 'teach you how to turn a heel?'

'She tried but I wasn't very good at it,' I admitted. 'She had to help me when I got to that bit.'

Agnes' eyes narrowed and she started muttering to herself, 'Maybe I should oughta go. Take the kid. I could now he's out the house.

That'd show 'em who's doin' what for the war victims. Me walkin' in with a real live British refugee kid. And one that knows knittin'. I need to think on that...'

SIX

Just as Agnes wouldn't put up with any of us walking when we could be running, neither would she put up with any 'gabbin'' from us, her word for talking.

She needn't have worried. Aside from her threats as to what she would do to us if she caught us gabbin' (her favourite being rinsing out our mouths with gasoline), we were, for the most part, a silent bunch of kids, far too fear-ridden to have any clear thoughts in our heads other than the ones she put there and therefore we never had anything to talk about.

Neither James nor I had any difficulty picturing ourselves as we would have appeared back then had there been anyone to see us: six grubby, barefoot little kids in ragged overalls running – always running – with hunched shoulders and anxious, frowning faces scampering about doing Agnes' bidding. We were far too preoccupied, too frightened, to ever enjoy a leisurely moment of laughter or engage in the usual 'kidding around' typical of kids our age. Not that there was anything to laugh at or kid around about.

Certainly James and I, our journey then behind us, had long since reverted to our customary lack of interest in one another, a habit Cathy and Danny seemed to share; while Andy and Sally could remain totally silent for days – sometimes weeks – at a time and often did. To the best of James' and my joint recollection then, none of the six of us ever once discussed or described our lives or families prior to arriving at 'this dump', the term that, without discussion, was our unanimous take on the Slater household.

It was quite natural, then, that the subject of Agnes' participation in a Knitting Bee had been forgotten by all, until one evening a week or so after the subject originally came up, when Agnes, abandoning her rocker, stomped into the kitchen where we girls were doing the supper dishes, pointed at me, and said, 'Put down that dishrag, girl, and go get cleaned up. You're goin' knittin' tonight. 'Bout time you done somethin' for the U. S. of A. seein' what all I'm doin' fo you.'

I tried to swallow the piece of gristle I had taken from the side of the Old Man's plate, choked instead, and fell off the little stool we stood on to reach the sink, all the while wondering what Agnes meant by, 'Go get cleaned up.'

Did she mean go out back and wash my face and hands? Or did she mean, go change my clothes? If so, into what? Clean overalls? A dress?

I looked at Cathy and Sally for help or direction but both had become fascinated with the plates in their hands, holding them up close to their faces as though deciphering secret codes, which could only mean they were trying to swallow their Old Man's leftovers before Agnes caught them.

Exasperated by my failure to move, or even blink, Agnes grabbed me by one ear and dragged me towards the stairs. 'I said, get cleaned up!' she roared. 'Put on a dress. Shoes. Socks. Get a brush through that hair...'

I ran upstairs and stood in front of the hall closet still not sure what to wear. 'A dress,' she'd said. But ... which dress? I knew no matter which one I chose, Agnes would hate it so I thought I might as well put on the one I liked best. One that an Aunty in England had passed on to me when her daughter outgrew it, but which Mummy had never liked, saying it was too fussy with all the lace and ribbons and bows.

Next, I pulled on shoes and socks and couldn't understand why my feet felt so peculiar until I remembered it was the first time I'd worn shoes since I'd arrived there. I also marvelled at how dirty – caked-mud-dirty – my feet and legs were until I also remembered I hadn't had a bath since I got there either.

As I've already mentioned, there was another room next to the bedroom we all shared in that house that no one was allowed to enter. Cathy peeked in once anyway and said it was very pretty.

'Why – how come – aren't we allowed to go in it?' I remember asking.

'Used to be when the Old Man and the boys slep' in it, we did. Had to go in and make the beds anyways,' Cathy answered. 'But when they moved out to the cabin, Agnes fixed it up special for when her girl, Betty, comes home on leave. She figured on making it a big surprise.'

'So ... was she?' I asked.

'Was she what?'

'Surprised?'

Cathy put on her everybody's-dumb-but-me face and said, 'Now how could she be surprised if'n she ain't never been out to see it?'

How was I supposed to know that?

Actually, I had seen parts of the room when Agnes occasionally left the door ajar and I hadn't thought it was that pretty. But now here she came up the stairs, pushing past me at the closet and opening the door to the forbidden room wide. She motioned me to follow her.

I saw there were curtains at the windows that matched the bedspread on the bed, and shiny brown linoleum covered the ancient, splintering floorboards. On top of the linoleum was one of those ugly round rugs of the kind people make out of rags. There were two pictures of angels on one of the walls and in a corner, a washstand with a frilly white skirt around it. I remember thinking if anybody fixed up a room like that as a surprise for me it would have been hard to pretend I liked it.

While I was looking around, Agnes pulled off her ugly old print dress and pulled on one that was all one colour, pink, with a crocheted collar. It was ugly, too, but at least it didn't have a hole under the arm.

'Get over here, button the buttons down my back,' she ordered, sitting on the edge of the bed, 'then go bring me the hairbrush here.'

Ugh! I cringed from touching that fat back of hers and it took me ages to button up her buttons because of trying to keep my fingers away from the sweat that beaded and trickled over its entire surface.

On the washstand in the corner, all arranged at angles, stood an array of china jugs and bowls and jars. They all matched: white with trailing red roses on the sides and gold trim around the top.

When I came back from our room with

the hairbrush, Agnes was wringing out a wash cloth in the biggest bowl and wiping her face and neck with it. She grabbed me and scrubbed my face and neck and the parts of my arms and legs that showed. When she dropped the cloth back in the bowl the water turned a rich, dark brown, something she noted with obvious satisfaction.

'My sailor boy, Jack, must've been right sayin' you Limeys was a filthy bunch with rats big as dogs runnin' around your ships,' she sneered, 'on account of take a look at that there water. There's your proof.'

I had learned by then not to answer when she said rude and nasty things about England or the English and handed her the hairbrush in silence. She dragged it through my dirty, tangled hair with a ferocity that made James' shipboard efforts seem downright friendly by comparison. I couldn't help but cry out and for every 'Ouch!' I earned a whack on the head from the back of the brush. By the time she was through, my eyes and nose were streaming and my skull was covered in lumps.

With all my heart I wished I'd learned from Cathy and kept my mouth shut. Particularly about knitting. Thanks to my loud, bragging talk, I was not only getting beat up, but was going to have to be alone with Agnes for the first time since my arrival and my heart was racing at the thought. What would she do to me? What would I say to her? Unexpectedly, the hated kitchen with its chipped dishes and worn-out furniture and linoleum took on the aspect of dear, familiar friends from which I could scarcely bear to be parted. As for Cathy and Sally, I couldn't imagine what it would be like for them to have some time without the ever-present fear of Agnes and her thumping fists to contend with. It didn't seem right. In fact, I thought it horribly unfair.

Outside, Agnes, gripping the back of my neck as though fearing I might make a run for it, silently steered me to a different path in the woods than the one we followed to the store. This path was the one the Old Man disappeared into when he left to catch his bus in the mornings. Did that mean we were going to take a bus?

No, it didn't. When we came out of the woods we continued to walk along a paved road and stayed on it until we came to a nice, big friendly house with a white picket fence and a pretty garden.

A smiling lady opened the door and introduced us to the seated knitters. 'Girls,' she trilled, 'our wonderful neighbour, Agnes here, is providing a home and shelter for this poor little British refugee child and she's brought her here tonight to help us knit.'

The ladies gasped and clapped and escorted Agnes to the best chair in the room and it was then I noticed a change in Agnes' behaviour towards me. Her grip – now on my arm – loosened and instead of hitting me on the head and calling me a Limey, her arm went around my shoulders in a gentle kind of way and she smiled down at me as if I was someone very dear to her. She even went so far as to call me honey and tell everyone what a perfect little lady I was.

The ladies – there were about twelve of them – kept up their praise of Agnes, telling her she was an example to them all. A fine, upstanding American if ever there was one.

Sitting beside her on a little stool the lady found for me and listening to them talk while carefully knitting, I suddenly knew with certainty that if my very own mother were to walk in just then and meet Agnes, she'd say the same as everyone else – that she was really quite a splendid woman. Remarkable, in fact. An example to them all.

Across the room from where I sat stood a table laden with the most wonderful-looking food I had seen in America. It reminded me of birthday party tables in England before the war with its cakes, pies, cupcakes, custards and biscuits – cookies – of the very best kind.

The lady who let us in came through from her kitchen cooing, 'Coffee's ready, girls! Come taste my goodies!'

Agnes and the other ladies set aside their knitting and headed for the table. It took Agnes a moment to remember me but when she did, she smiled and held out her hand. I was only too happy to smile back and take it and go to the table with her.

The kind lady said, 'Help yourself, honey,' and before I knew it I had put two of everything on my plate. Then I remembered Agnes and, gulping, hastened to put some back. Agnes' hand on my shoulder stopped me.

'It's OK, honey,' she smiled. 'Eat up! We all know what you been through in England with the rationing: but the one egg a month; people lining up all day and all night for a couple potatoes... Eat!'

The ladies, aghast at Agnes' comments, likewise urged me on. 'Take more!' they said. 'Eat! Here, take a slice of this pie and try some of these cookies. They're homemade, you know!'

One particularly sweet lady reached out to pat my head. I pulled away, wincing, because her hand had landed on a couple of Agnes' hairbrush lumps. The lady saw the lumps and gasped, 'My land, child, what's all this?'

I knew better than to say Agnes did it with the hairbrush. What, and risk the lady getting mad at me like Bill had done? Hear her say I must be a very bad kid indeed to try the patience of an upstanding woman like Agnes to where she had to hit me! I tried to think where to say the lump came from but Agnes stepped in and lied for me.

'Sarah can't keep out the way of our screen doors,' she said, laughing convulsively.

The ladies didn't laugh. They didn't know what she was talking about. Neither did I.

Agnes explained. 'They don't got 'em over there, see. Screen doors. That's how come she walks into every last one. She don't see they're there. I keep telling her to mind but, you know kids, always in a hurry to get outside and play.'

Ah! Now they understood. Chuckling with delight, they murmured, 'Oh, Agnes! You're so good!'

Agnes relished being the centre of attention with everyone laughing at her sparkling wit and she lied some more. 'That brother of hers is the same way! I swear there's days the both of them look like they come through Germany!'

The ladies howled at that.

Agnes' kind-hearted benevolence shut down the moment our hostess's front door closed on our backs. I was berated all the way home through the dark woods for eating too much, talking too much, and because, under the lamplight, the parting in my hair had shown my scalp to be the same filthy brown my legs had been.

'Shamed the living life out of me is what you done,' Agnes spluttered. 'Next time I tell you get cleaned up, you better do it right.'

I worried for days about how I was going to get my scalp clean for the next meeting. I'd never washed my own hair before but I knew I would need shampoo. Where could I get some? Or would soap do? But there again, where could I get soap? Or could Cathy maybe just wash my parting with plain old water? Down at the well?

Cathy said, 'I ain't gettin' my head busted open on account of you. What you need to do next meetin' is quick go sit in a dark corner where there ain't no lamp. Like that no one'll see the top of your head.'

That was a good idea that Cathy had.

Right after breakfast the morning after the Knitting Bee, Agnes sent me out to the side porch to knit. I was to finish a pair of socks before next week's meeting, or else...

The other kids hated the sight of me sitting knitting while they took on my share of the daily chores. Even James looked surly when he passed the porch with one of the cows or a wagon-load of cow pies to throw on the vegetables.

'You wouldn't think it was so wonderful if you had to do it just once,' I told them when we were all washing our hands at the outside basin. 'Right after breakfast when it's still

106

cool and I'm not too hungry,' I continued, 'it's not so bad. But what about later, huh? What about when the sun comes to take away the shade and blinds my eyes and my tummy aches on account of it's so empty?

'And how about when I'm so hot and thirsty I think I'll die. Or when I need to go to the shit house or I need to get up and walk around because – on account of – I've got pins and needles in my feet and Agnes says stay put till she says otherwise? Do you know,' I always concluded, 'how long "otherwise" takes to get here?'

They didn't want to know.

'Still beats bein' in the kitchen with her beatin' up on you with whatever she's got in her hand,' Cathy glowered.

'Unh-unh,' I argued. 'You're wrong because in the kitchen you're fixin' food so even with her beating up on you, you get a chance to stick bits of bruised fruit or apple peels in your pocket when her back's turned. But out on the porch there's nothing. Just that hot, hot, sun and Agnes shouting – yelling – at me through the screen door.

'You turned that heel yet, girl?'

'No, ma'am.'

'No heel, no lunch.'

'Yes, ma'am.'

Every day I wondered why the silly old fool had to yell? Couldn't she see that her yelling startled me and that's what made me drop stitches? Not only did dropped stitches get me a beating but with the beating came the threat that she wouldn't take me to the next meeting. An alarming threat indeed, for I had already come to think about the laden tables at those meetings the way I used to think about the candy case in Bill's store.

Something else the kids hated even more than seeing me knit was hearing me talk about all the wonderful, delicious food that was always served. The last time I started to describe it, Cathy told me to shut up.

'I'm plain wore out listenin' to you,' she complained. ''Sides, me'n Sally gets candy knittin' nights, too, and we don't have to go no place with old Agnes to get it neither.'

Right away I knew she was lying because I knew there wasn't any candy in the house and that's what I told her.

Just as smug as can be, tossing her head like little Miss Priss, she replied, 'I ain't sayin' no more. I ain't s'posed to tell about it anyways but you better get that damn sock done. We're countin' on you keepin' Agnes out the house so we can get our candy. And if you don't finish, you'll have more'n old Agnes beatin' up on you. You'll have me'n Sally right alongside her.'

Puh! As if I cared about them.

Far more worrying was the fact that every once in a while my mind would wander of its own accord and I would drop a stitch through my own carelessness. What was up-setting about that – frightening, even – was that when I did, Agnes somehow always knew about it and would come storming through the screen door to snatch the knit-ting away with one hand, slap my head with the other and point to the vegetable field.

'Git!' she'd holler. 'Go pull weeds. The others done et your lunch anyways on ac-count of they been doin' your work and all you done is set drop stitches all mornin' long.'

To console myself on the way to the field, I would tell myself, So what! I don't care. I won't pull a single weed when I get there. Well ... maybe just enough to kneel on so my knees won't blister on that hot, hot dirt. But after that, I won't. No, sir! I'll just sit perfectly still and pretend I'm in Bill's store picking out candy.

One day when I had been sent to the field for dropping a stitch I heard the screen door slam and I started pulling weeds as if I could win a prize for it, thinking it was Agnes coming to check on me.

But it turned out to be just Cathy and Sally and Sally was crying and rubbing her head so I knew Agnes had been at her with her fists. When they got closer, I saw the sides of Cathy's face were flaming red, too, but she wasn't crying. I realized then that I'd never ever seen Cathy cry. Not one single time.

When they got close enough for me to hear, Cathy yelled, 'How come you can't never do nothin' right, huh? Old Agnes has been beatin' up on all of us on account of you droppin' that damn stitch!'

'I didn't do it on purpose,' I yelled back. 'Agnes scares me coming out the door the way she does and anyway, I'd like to see you knitting. You'd be a lot worse at it than me.'

Right away Cathy put on her slitty-eyed look. 'Ain't nothin' you can do I can't do better,' she jeered. 'And you better get that sock done so she takes you knittin' next time else you know what you can expect from me.'

Just then I had the best idea I'd had in my whole life and it was my turn to go slitty-eyed. I said, 'You don't tell me where you get candy knittin' nights I won't finish that sock on purpose and that's what you can expect from me.'

That stopped her! Her mouth dropped open and Sally looked like she was going to start crying all over again.

Cathy got hold of herself. 'He gives it us,' she said. 'Him. The Old Man.'

I looked at Sally and saw she was holding her hair back from her face with both hands so I could see it and nodding her head, saying, 'Yeah. It's the Old Man gives it us.'

I didn't believe either one of them and said so. 'Him?' I jeered. 'He don't even come in the house 'cept but to eat.'

'He can if he wants,' Cathy screeched. 'He's a grown-up, ain't he? Grown-ups can do anythin' they feel like and if he feels like comin' in the house knittin' nights that's what he's gonna do. That first time he come over me'n Sally was sayin' our Hail Marys and we heard him callin' out our names. We got up to look and he was standin' at the bottom of the stairs in his stockin' feet, a Milky Way bar in each hand.'

All I could think to say back was, 'Milky Way bars...' in a kind of moan, Milky Way bars, at that time, being my most favourite candy. Maybe Cathy was telling the truth then? If she'd been lying she'd have just said candy, right? I mean, like any old candy.

Cathy's eyes went all dreamy as if she was remembering how they tasted. 'Yeah,' she said. 'Milky Way bars. And he told us come on down get one. One at a time though on account of keepin' a eye out for you all comin' back. I went first on account of I'm the oldest and the biggest and he picked me up and hugged me and said he knowed me'n Sally was good girls even if Agnes din't. Then he sat me on his knee and rocked me.'

'He rocked you? In her rocking chair?'

'I just told you! 'Course in her rockin' chair. Ain't no other I ever saw.'

I was silent a long moment while pictures of what she had told me drifted through my

111

head and then I asked, 'So then what happened?'

'Din't nothin' happen. When I got done eatin' my candy bar he said it was Sally's turn and give him some goodnight kisses and go get her.'

Ugh! I remembered how I'd hated it when I was a little kid in England and told to kiss all the hairy, smelly old aunts and uncles who came to tea.

'Poor you,' I said. 'I hate kissing grownups.'

Cathy nodded. 'Me, too!' She even shuddered. She said, 'He stinks! And his mouth's awful big and awful wet and he sticks his tongue inside our mouths between our teeth and don't never want to quit. But he says "No kisses, no candy bars next time, so..."' she shrugged, 'we go ahead and let him kiss us.'

'I wouldn't,' I said. 'I'd run away and hide.'

'Like heck you would. I know darn well you like Milky Way bars bad as us.'

She was right. I did. And I wondered how to get him to give me one without kissing him.

'Next Saturday,' I began, 'when he's home, I'll ask him for one and when he asks for a kiss I'll tell him I got to go because – on account of – I hear Agnes calling my name.'

'You know well as I do he don't talk to none

112

of us when she's around,' Cathy said, using her, how-come-I-have-to-explain-everything tone of voice. 'That's why we need for you to finish that sock and go knittin' with her. 'Sides, soon's he gets done deliverin' the Saturday chickens, he'll pass out drunk till Monday mornin' like always, so how're you gonna ask, huh?'

I didn't answer because I didn't know but I was certain I'd think of something.

SEVEN

Even with a forty-year interval between our 'now' and our 'then', James still paled visibly when we got around to the Saturday morning routine at the Slaters'. 'God, how I always dreaded it,' he groaned.

'Guts and feathers day,' was how Danny used to describe it.

'More like, stink and gag day,' Cathy would argue.

They were both right. Saturday was the day we killed and dressed the chickens the Old Man took orders for at his workplace during the week. Regardless of the number ordered – anywhere from ten to fifteen – we had to have them all ready and packed up in time for him to catch the noon bus to town and make his deliveries, trailing with him the combined stench of wood smoke, blood, steaming piles of guts and wet feathers that clung to all of us.

Next to Monday, wash day, Saturday was the day we kids dreaded most at the Slaters'. Saturdays meant the six of us working alongside the sweating, screaming, stinking Agnes the whole morning long and we were agreed that if there was one thing worse than getting beat up and jeered at yourself, it was standing by while she berated someone else. It made you feel ashamed you were too little and too afraid to stick up for the victim, while filling your already bursting heart with ever more hatred and contempt for her.

We ate our cornflakes standing up Saturday mornings and left the dishes in the sink for later. Then, with fast-beating hearts and lowered eyes, we lined up and followed Agnes outside.

'You boys get that incinerator goin', get water heatin',' she'd begin. 'Girls, get in the run, start catchin'.' Shading her eyes with one hand, she'd begin pointing with the other, 'I want that 'un ... n' that 'un ... n' that 'un...'

It's not easy keeping your eyes on just one chicken when you consider all chickens look alike. And forget about chickens being stupid. On the contrary, the minute we opened the gate to their run they knew exactly why

114

we were there and in panicked frenzy, pooping as they ran, headed for a corner where they created, of themselves, a monstrous heap, the object of each being to be buried on the bottom. You could always count on yours being the first to achieve that goal.

To catch your chicken you had to devise a way to separate it from the others, chase it into a different corner – never mind if you slipped and fell in the poop – and then throw yourself on top of it. There was no other way.

Try to grab one on the run and all you got was a handful of feathers and Agnes screaming, 'You miss one more time, girl, and I'll see you in jail alongside that fool mother of yours that's been locked up since the day you got born.'

If you were Cathy, you heard about the colour of your hair, something Agnes could never forgive her. 'Whatever loony give birth to you must've dyed your hair that goldie colour 'fore they took and locked her up for good and that's where you're going, girl, the booby hatch, you don't catch that bird right quick.'

Sometimes two of us got our chickens headed towards the same corner and, intent on our mission and unaware of the other, collided and knocked ourselves nearly senseless as we hurled ourselves upon our victims. That really got Agnes in a frenzy, especially if one of the two was Sally who ran around inside the pens with her eyes tight shut underneath her flopping hair.

Poor little Sally. Not only was she still a baby, only just turned five, but she was also terrified – scared to death – of chickens. So scared she'd wake us all up at night, most particularly Friday nights, the sheets and her underpants soaked through, screaming about chickens coming at her with their beaks wide open and their claws in her eyes.

'Beats us how you can be scared of a dumb-ass chicken when you got Agnes outside the fence hollerin' about how she's gonna hang you upside down by your feet on the clothes line alongside them dead chickens,' was what the rest of us told her. Sally stayed scared anyway.

Once you had your chicken firmly clasped under one arm you groped for its feet – those clawing, frantic feet – and carried it upside down to Agnes at the gate. She passed it along to Danny who, like a miniature executioner, stood at the chopping block, axe at the ready. Severing the head with one blow, he would hand the convulsing body to James.

Because he was the tallest, it fell to James to hang the headless chickens by their feet to one of the clothes lines so their blood would drain out. That wasn't as easy as it sounds because although the chickens were headless, their bodies didn't know it. Their legs kept trying to run, their wings kept flapping, and their blood, spewing from the neck stump at his eye level as he tried to secure them, blinded him.

On one particularly frightening Saturday Agnes grabbed a caught chicken from Cathy and thrust it at James instead of Danny. 'I've about had enough of your sissy ways, boy,' she glowered, 'always hangin' back lettin' the others do your share of the work.'

Yanking the axe away from Danny, she shoved it into James' free hand, lined him up at the chopping block and roared, 'Kill it!'

James took a big, deep breath and closed his eyes. Agnes went ballistic. 'Open your eyes, boy!' she hollered. 'Jesus! No wonder you Limeys can't win your goddamn war if'n you all run around with your eyes tight shut.'

James opened his eyes, took another deep breath, raised both arms together, the crazed, flapping bird in one hand, the bloody axe in the other, brought them down together and … no one could believe it! The chicken's head fell off, landing smack in the middle of the pile of heads already severed by Danny.

There was a great buzzing from the flies come to gorge on the bloody heads and there was James, all surprised and amazed, turning to see if Agnes had actually seen what he had done while doubtless hoping she'd give him a smile or say something nice. Something like, 'Well done!' or, 'Gee whiz!'

Forget it. Somehow or other he had done

something wrong and Agnes was even madder than before. She grabbed the convulsing chicken away from him, hit him on the side of the head with it – both sides, actually – and blood splattered everywhere.

'I ain't about to have no sissy Limey boy smirkin' at me out the sides o' his eyes,' she roared. 'From now on you leave the killin' to Danny, him being a real boy, and you get in the pens with the girls where you belong.'

Poor James. No one could look at him. We knew he felt ashamed and scared and desperate all at the same time and that, more than anything, he yearned for revenge. Revenge of the kind we dreamed up on the rare occasions Agnes neglected to keep us separated.

In those fantasies, Agnes, already starved and desperate with thirst, was sent to catch every chicken in the run. When she had caught every last one, we let them all out and made her start again. When she caught them all a second time, we smeared her with blood, draped her in guts and hung her by her feet on the clothes line. Not just for an hour or a day, but until she died. We felt pretty confident that would shut her up. But good...

Once the blood stopped dripping out of the chickens the boys would take them down and bring them over to the table where we girls were waiting to pluck them.

To pluck a chicken properly you have to

first loosen its feathers by dousing the entire bird in the bucket of water the boys had set to heat earlier.

When Agnes' back was turned, Cathy would hiss dousing instructions to Sally and me since our only skill in that direction seemed to centre on severely scalding our own hands and feet.

'You got to hold on tight to their feet,' Cathy would hiss, 'and put 'em in head first else how you gonna get the wings in, huh? Jesus! Now pull it out! Quick! They stay in too long they start cookin'!'

No sooner had we done exactly what she said than she was hissing the reverse. 'You're taking 'em out too soon! You take 'em out too soon, the feathers don't come out good. And mind you get all them little bitty pin feathers too, hear, else you'll have Agnes comin' at you with the hatchet!'

After the plucking, Agnes cut the chickens' backsides open and pulled out their steaming innards. 'Guttin',' she called it. Lastly she cut off their feet and set them aside for our nightly soup.

It was Cathy's job to pull the gizzards, hearts and livers – giblets, Agnes called them – out of the steaming piles of guts, rinse them, and put a set back in each bird.

On this particular Saturday, Agnes was in the act of cutting open yet another chicken when her head went down, her eyes closed

119

and she was holding on to the edge of the plucking table with both hands.

Jesus, our eyes telegraphed one another, she's havin' another one of them dizzy spells! Dizzy spells being the latest thing Cathy had warned us about. One more item on the growing list of things Agnes didn't used to have or do that were making her a little bit worse every day.

This one went on longer than usual, though, and we were beginning to fidget from staying still so long – we always stood motionless while Agnes 'had her a spell' – when she took a deep breath, straightened up and told Cathy to take over. 'I ain't feelin' right,' she gasped. 'I need to go on up the house, set a spell.'

We all knew better than to look at her or say anything, and we didn't. Not until we heard the back screen door slam at which time we all started talking at once.

'Door slammin' don't mean for sure she's inside!' Cathy barked. 'She coulda done it to fool us. Be hidin' ... waitin' with the strap...'

We stopped our chatter instantly but we looked at each other sideways, all thinking the same thing: There she goes bossing again. Damn, but she's worse even than Agnes.

Striding to where Agnes had stood at the table, Cathy took up an Agnes-like stance and barked her first order to the boys: They was to quit with the killing. 'We got enough,' she said, finished with her counting. 'Need you to go build up that fire in the incinerator for the guts and feathers.'

The boys pulled taunting, ugly faces at her but, while taking their time about it, did as she told them. Turning to Sally, Cathy ordered her, on a high note of exasperation, to quit scratching the bug bites on her arms.

'You can't see all you're doin' is smear blood every which way?' she asked. 'An' what's that gonna do but make more bugs come'n bite you.'

Sally's bottom lip pushed out – I could see it through the curtain of hair hanging over her face – and she kept right on scratching.

Cathy exploded. 'I swear old Agnes is right!' she raged. 'Ain't nothin' gone right around here since Annie and Billy got took away and we got you bunch of sorry crybabies instead.' She glared at us and we glared right back.

'I wish Annie was here right now!' she raged on. 'She could gut and pluck a chicken faster even than Agnes. The way you're goin' at it we ain't never gonna get these birds done by noon.'

Loud enough for Cathy to hear, I said to Sally, 'There she goes again with her Annie and Billy stories and you know she makes 'em up. I bet there never even was an Annie and a Billy. I bet she made them up, too. To scare us.'

121

Cathy heard me just as I knew she would. 'I did not!' she howled, her eyes watering with anger. 'Annie and Billy was the first foster kids Agnes ever took in and they was big. Annie was only just turned eleven but she already had grown-up titties. And Billy wasn't but ten and near as tall as the Old Man. They could do everythin' better'n us little kids.'

I wondered why Agnes sent them away if they were so big and so wonderful. 'Did their Mummy and Daddy come and take them away?' I asked.

Pursing her lips, Cathy said, 'No, their Mum-my and Dad-dy didn't come and take them away. Old crazy Bennings did.'

'Well ... what'd she do that for if Agnes liked them so much?'

Cathy didn't know. 'I'm still tryin' to figure that one out,' she complained. 'All I know is Agnes and her sister Martha – she's the one I told you used to come visit back then – was fightin' real bad one time and Aunt Martha told Agnes she needed to get rid of all the girls on account of what if he got after them like he done Annie and they all ended up gettin' babies.'

What? Annie got a baby? 'You mean a real one?' I gasped. 'An alive one?'

'That's somethin' else I still ain't figured on account of I never saw Annie with no baby,' Cathy said. 'All I know is Agnes told

Aunt Martha the girls was stayin' put bein' kids and farmin' was the only way she knew to make a buck and how was she supposed to get done fixin' the place over and sellin' for a profit without them to help out?

'Aunt Martha said, "That's easy. Just take in boys."'

'"They won't let me," Agnes replied. "I already tried. I gotta take what they send. Anybody's leavin," she finished up, "it's him."

'Aunt Martha said, "How you fixin' to work that one out, huh? You fixin' on puttin' a bullet in him?"'

A bullet? At those words I stopped plucking and Sally stopped scratching. Together, we asked, 'Who? Who was she fixin' to put a bullet in?'

Cathy shrugged. 'Had to have been the Old Man she was talkin' about on account of she told Aunt Martha he was fixin' up the old cabin back in the woods and wouldn't be comin' in the house no more 'cept but to eat. Turns out that's what he done.

'Aunt Martha said if Agnes believed that and that's how it was gonna be, count on never seein' her out here no more and she up and left and never has come back.'

Sally started scratching again. 'Wisht I could find me a baby so Bennings'd come get me,' she sighed.

Even as she spoke those words, I remembered asking my mother once where people got babies from and her saying they found them under gooseberry bushes. I passed the information on.

Sally stopped her scratching again and pushed her hair out of her face and I could see she was laughing. 'Heck,' she said, 'if that's all you gotta do, let's go find one right now! What they look like, them kind of bushes?'

I couldn't remember! I knew they had prickles on them but I couldn't remember anything else because it had been so long since I'd seen one. 'Maybe they don't grow in America?' I ventured.

'They got to, else how come Annie found her one?' Cathy reasoned. 'Bet what happens is Agnes pulls 'em up whenever she finds 'em on account of her hatin' babies like she does. That's how come Annie got took away and that's how come she hates the both of you. 'Cause you're babies.'

'I ain't no baby!' Sally glowered.

'Me, either,' I said. 'Ain't a person alive can't see I'm a heck of a lot bigger than you.'

'Bigger don't make you smarter,' Cathy sneered. 'Only birthdays do that and I'm goin' on nine. That's how come she makes me boss over all you dumb little kids.'

In England kids weren't allowed to hit one another, but in the Slater household we could hit each other whenever we felt like it and I was just going to smack Cathy as hard

124

as I could for being such a bossy twerp when a big gust of wind blew across the yard and the feathers we'd plucked started flying everywhere. Next, the prop holding the chicken house door open fell down with a clatter and the door started slamming itself against the side of the building.

'Go fix that door right now 'fore Agnes comes out fixes you,' Cathy yelled to the boys.

'Go fix it yourself, Agnes!' Danny yelled back.

Cathy didn't hear him. She was looking up at the sky that had turned black and at the feathers flying and the trees bending and she was worried. 'We got to get a move on!' she said. 'Looks like we got us a big storm comin'.'

She turned her attention to the drawn-shades, closed-door house. 'It ain't like her goin' on up there like she done it being Saturday and him home and all these chickens to get ready,' she muttered. Louder, she said, 'Bet she's layin' down in Betty's room again. Last couple of times she sent me in there to clean the bed was all mussed up.'

'I wish she'd sleep in there all the time 'stead of next to me,' I glowered. 'She sure stinks!'

Sally looked hopeful. 'You figure she might could be dyin'?' she asked. 'That old dog was here when me'n Andy first come didn't do nothin' but lay around all the time till we figured out it was dead.'

'That old dog died 'cause she never give it nothin' to eat,' Cathy said. 'Kept all the leftovers for them hogs of hers. Nah, Agnes ain't dyin'. She might could be sick, though, on account of them dizzy spells she keeps gettin' and her back all the time hurtin' her. That, or she's got lost in her picture box again.'

Agnes had a cigar box that she carried with her everywhere, most particularly to the shit house. Cathy peeked inside it once and told us it was full of pictures Agnes cut out of newspapers and old magazines. Pictures of brand new bathrooms and kitchens with electric stoves and all kinds of other modern things Agnes wanted. 'Stuff,' Cathy elaborated, 'she's plannin' to buy just as soon as she gets done fixin' this place over and sellin' for a profit. Agnes hates this dump worse even than us,' she concluded.

'How do you know?' I asked.

'I know 'cause that's what I heard her tell Aunt Martha back when she used to come visit.'

Cathy got bossy again, calling the boys over to help with the plucking. 'We don't get these chickens done 'fore that rain gets here,' she warned, 'we might could all get tied up kneeling on the porch all night with a storm goin' on... Nothin' to eat...'

I reminded her Agnes said she wanted

rain. 'Ever since James and I got here she's been saying it was our fault it wasn't raining so maybe now she'll be happy,' I said.

That shut Cathy up. It even made her smile. For about half a minute. 'Yeah!' she said. 'Rain might could put her in a good mood.'

Agnes' moods were everyone's day-long obsession. From the first sidelong glances, stolen at dawn as we sidled past her with the night-pot, or set the table for breakfast, to the last scurry upstairs at night, we attempted to gauge her state of mind. And when any one of us girls set foot outside, no matter the time of day or the direction in which we headed, there was always a boy lurking to ask from the side of his mouth, 'She in a good mood?'

I used to wonder why they kept asking since none of us had ever once said, 'Yep! She's in a good one.' I even wondered how we would know because I was certain I'd never seen her have one.

In a short while it did start to rain and soon after that we all went in the barn and shut the door because it was coming down so hard it was blowing inside and making puddles on the dirt floor.

'We let them sacks of chicken feed get wet forget about lunch and supper,' Cathy began on a new litany. 'Forget about settin' down for a week. Forget about–'

Danny told her to shut up and after that

we all sat silent, too hungry and too worried to do anything else.

The Old Man stopped by after a while and without saying a word to any of us took the chickens away to wherever it was he took them and still there was no sign of Agnes. Cathy was worried sick about that but the rest of us weren't. Before we got too hungry to even talk, Danny said, 'The way it's comin' down right now I don't see us needin' to haul for a week. Don't worry, though, she'll find us worse stuff, more'n likely. Like emptying out the shit house...'

'Je-sus!' James exclaimed, pausing a moment to admire the way he sounded cussing, before asking, 'She makes us do that?'

'Damn right,' came the answer.

I could see James thinking about asking how but deciding he'd rather not know. Danny enlightened him anyway. 'What you do,' he began, 'is lift up that back trap door and lower a bucket like as if you were down at the well. You tilt it so it fills up with shit and then you take and empty it in a hole she already had you dig way back deep in the woods. What you gotta watch out for is–'

There was a noise outside! Someone was trying to get the door open! We scrambled to our feet just as the door swung open showing us Agnes, drenched, trying to catch her breath and see us in the dark, both at the same time.

'Them chickens,' she gasped, 'They done?'

We all nodded our heads knowing the first one to speak would be the one most likely to get punched.

'Well, don't stand there gawkin',' Agnes snapped. 'Show me!'

'Um ... Mr Slater, ma'am...' Cathy mumbled. 'He done took 'em away. 'Bout an hour ago.'

Because of the gloom, we couldn't see Agnes' face clearly but we could tell, from the way her head went up, the way she gasped, that she was mad. 'You tellin' me you let him go off to town without me lookin' 'em over?'

Head bowed, Cathy nodded.

'You wash 'em off good? Get out the pin feathers? Pack in the giblets?'

Heads coming up, we all nodded, proud to have done everything exactly right.

Agnes stood quiet a minute trying to think of something else to get mad about. It didn't take long.

'Them feathers,' she shrieked, 'You never burned the feathers. Whole damn place is covered in 'em.'

Danny spoke up. 'We was gonna, ma'am, only he – Mr Slater, ma'am – said to wait on it. Said we'd have the whole place on fire in this wind.'

'Not-a-one of you smart enough to tell him rain is water and water puts out fires?' Agnes sneered.

We'd have sneered right back if we'd dared and told her that was why we didn't build up the fire – rain puts them out. But we knew better and stood in front of her the safest way we knew how – heads hanging low and not a word out of any of us.

A sudden clatter on the tin roof told us the rain was gaining strength and it gave Agnes something new to yell about. 'Now look what you done,' she fumed. 'Got me stuck out here in the barn with trash like you-all. Jesus! Did you check them rain barrels was under the spouts?'

Together, the boys chorused, 'Yes, ma'am!'

'Soon's we saw the storm comin',' Danny bragged, and knew right away he should have kept his mouth shut because he was the one to get the first punch.

'You ain't none of you lollygaggin' around down here all day doin' nothin',' Agnes said when she'd had enough of punching Danny. 'Plenty for you to do up at the house.'

Grabbing a feed sack from a pile near the door, she threw it over her head and led the dash to the kitchen.

Once inside, all of us drenched, covered in dirt and chicken blood and worrying what might come next, we lined up in a row before Agnes and studied her carefully.

From the way she was pacing and pulling on her bottom lip, we could tell she didn't know what to do with us. She stopped, sniffed, made a face, 'You all stink!' she glowered, eyeing us with distaste. That gave her an idea and she brightened. 'Baths!' she yelped. 'You need 'em and now I got rain pourin' down I can spare the water for once. You boys go get more wood, so I can build up the fire. Cathy, run upstairs get clean overalls and underwear for you girls. Sally, run on over to the cabin get clean stuff for the boys.'

As had happened before, I was the one left sitting on the bench with no instructions. I sat very still and tried to look at the floor – it was always the safest place to look – but my eyes kept straying to the table where a fly was busy crawling over the leftovers from the Old Man's lunch sandwich.

While I watched, it came out from between two crusts of bread, sat itself down on a sliver of tomato and began the busy business of washing its face. Agnes' back was turned and, scaring myself nearly breathless even while I moved, I grabbed those crusts, stuffed them in my pocket and was back sitting on the bench, all in the time it had taken Agnes to throw a handful of sticks on the fire.

Soft as a whisper, Agnes said, 'Bring them crusts here to me, girl.'

The room seemed to blur and sway as I crept across the floor towards her. When I drew alongside, she lifted the lid off the stove, threw in the crusts, and screeched with laughter as I leapt back from the uncovered flames roaring out of the opening.

With an effort, Agnes controlled herself and even quieter than before, said, 'Nobody ever tell you stealin's a sin?'

I was so frightened – scared – my legs were shaking and I couldn't say a word, not even 'Yes, ma'am'.

Agnes smiled her soft, tender smile, 'Give me your hand,' she crooned.

As if mesmerized, my eyes held fast by hers, I held out my hand. Agnes grabbed it, started lowering it to the flames...

There came a sudden loud crash from the office next door. A scream. The smile dropped from Agnes' face. Cursing, she flung me aside and strode into the office. I heard another crash, a yelp, and Cathy, clearly propelled by a blow from Agnes, came flying through the door, to be brought up short by the kitchen table.

'I couldn't help it, ma'am,' she whimpered. 'I couldn't see nothin'. It's awful dark on them stairs and in the office what with the storm and all–'

Agnes' hand was raised to strike again when her face changed. She looked from Cathy to me frowning and we knew she was trying to remember what she'd set out to do. We felt hopeful. Maybe she'd forget the time? She did once. Maybe she'd give us lunch? Our hopes were short lived. 'Baths...'

Agnes muttered. '...was gonna make 'em take baths.' She strode into the bathroom – a room that wasn't a bathroom at all, just an alcove off the kitchen with a bath tub in it – a tub with no water supply and no drain, which meant both clean and dirty water had to be carried in and out in buckets as we knew from emptying Agnes' once monthly bath – and called to us to bring in the water.

We filled three buckets with the steaming, rust-coloured water from the tank on the back of the range and carried them into the bathroom. Agnes smiled her most loving smile, 'Go ahead and put the plug in the drain now, Sarah,' she crooned.

I froze. The plug? What plug? How could she expect me to know where she kept the plug? I never saw it before. Never had a bath here before. I looked at Cathy and Sally but they were staring at the floor just as I would have if I'd been them.

Agnes purred, 'Looks like I'm going to have to use the strap 'less Miss England here finds that plug pretty damn quick.' She headed for the door. 'Find it or else,' she warned, and the door slammed shut behind her.

Cathy ran to the window set high in the wall, stood on tiptoe, felt along the ledge with her fingers, held out a plug.

I gasped. 'Is that it?'

Cathy nodded.

'Go give it to her quick 'fore she comes

back with the strap!'

Cathy sighed, 'Ain't you never gonna learn? She knows where it's at. She was lookin' right at it the whole time she was talkin'. She don't want us to find it. She wants to. You tell her you did, then it's her looks crazy. I think we oughta...' she stopped, shook her head. She didn't know.

'I'm gonna tell her you found it,' Sally said.

Cathy slapped her hand away from the door knob. 'No, you ain't!' she hissed. 'You go out there now her actin' like she is, ain't no tellin' what-all she might could do to you. Us...'

We stared at one another a long, long time, each striving to fathom Agnes' unfathomable mind.

Cathy decided to put the plug back on the ledge. 'Make like we're lookin' for it,' she instructed. 'Get down on your knees and feel around the floor.'

No sooner were we on our knees than the door rattled open and Agnes stood over us. She called back to the boys, 'Come in here take a look at these fool sisters of yours! All three of 'em crawlin' around the floor lookin' for the plug when the damn thing's right here on the ledge in front of their eyes!'

The boys knew exactly how to act. Crowding in the doorway they shook their heads in a sad, pitying kind of way at the sight of their crazy sisters crawling around the floor like the fools Agnes said they were. They did a good job. Agnes was so pleased she even smiled a real smile. Could she be getting in a good mood?

Nope, not a chance.

Reaching for the plug, Agnes put it in the drain and ordered us girls to strip down and get in the tub. Scalding hot water from the buckets cascaded down on us and then Agnes' hands were everywhere scrubbing an arm here, a leg there, a head of hair, a foot, a hand, all of it done with the brush we used to scrub the floors and the greasy, home-made lye soap Cathy said Agnes boiled up back of the barn once a year.

We were banished upstairs after our scrubbing where Sally cried herself to sleep even though we could hear the boys howling downstairs as if they were next door.

'You think she'll come after us anymore today?' I gulped to Cathy, fingering the blisters across my shoulders.

Cathy gave up squinting at her own blisters long enough to say, 'Nah. She'll be all wore out time she gets done with them boys. She'll be headin' for her rocker.'

For once Cathy was wrong.

From the bottom of the stairs, sounding so close we went rigid with fear, Agnes growled, 'Want you girls down here right now.'

We pulled Sally's sleep-drugged body off

the bed and half carried, half dragged her down the stairs.

Agnes was waiting for us in the kitchen, the boys, still wet and red from their scrubbing, lined up beside her. 'Seems like you-all forgot somethin',' she purred.

'To eat lunch, ma'am?' Danny suggested.

'Eat? You ain't got time to eat! Jesus! Do I have to think for you, too? The feathers! You forgot them feathers layin' out there like trash all over my land. Go get 'em. I find one feather time I come checkin' I'll ... I'll put you all in the incinerator alongside of 'em and have me a real fire!'

EIGHT

Every once in a while, Agnes – without ever meaning to, of course – did us kids a favour. She did the evening of the day I just recounted. In that instance, she yelled at the Old Man all the way through supper, thereby distracting herself enough to forget us completely. For the first time in weeks we were able to eat our small portions of food before she could snatch them away and fling them in the hog slops.

She began her tirade by berating him for taking off to deliver the chickens without

136

telling her. 'Leaving a pack of no-count brats runnin' wild fixin' to burn the whole entire place down lightin' fires.'

She moved on to his forgetting the butter she'd had Cathy churn the night before and the eggs she'd had Sally and me sort.

'How'm I supposed to keep customers, you don't deliver what-all I promise?' she wanted to know.

We were clearing the table and doing the dishes when she got around to the aggravation she had suffered giving us all baths, adding she wasn't planning on doing that no more.

'No, sir,' she said. 'Not even if Bennings calls and says she's comin' out. What I'll tell her and anyone else wants to know is, "How'm I s'posed to keep myself and six kids clean, never mind the cookin' and the cleanin' and the wash with no runnin' water on the place? You can't figure for yourself that's how come your own kids don't come near?' she raged. 'Why would they bein' they ain't got no place to wash their hands, even, and only that stinkin' shit-hole out back when they got to go?'

Whenever Agnes took on the Old Man, it always comforted James and me to know that no matter how wild her accusations, he would sit through them all in silence. At the same time it was something I, personally, could not understand. How was it, I wondered, that in this house Agnes was the bully while in my family, and in the families of many of my friends, it had always been the man – the Daddy – who was the bully?

'He don't talk back at her no more on account of he's scared of her,' was Cathy's opinion.

'How could he be scared of her?' I gasped. 'He's way bigger'n her?'

'He used to talk back at her once in a while,' Cathy said, 'but not since Annie and Billy got took away. I figure it's on account of he's scared Agnes will tell his own kids what he done to Annie – she's always saying she will – even though for the life of me I still ain't figured out what it was he done.'

Getting into bed that night, Cathy warned, 'We got to say the rosary like always in case Agnes shuts up her yelling long enough to listen.'

Sally and I pulled faces at her and remained silent.

'Go ahead then, get beat up,' Cathy said and started praying by herself. She'd just begun the second decade of the rosary when the door between the kitchen and the office banged open and we heard the Old Man talking on the telephone. Gasping, Cathy forgot all about her Hail Marys and her Our Fathers and dived for the top of the stairs. 'All the while I been here,' she marvelled in a whisper, 'I ain't never once heard him talk on the telephone. Not one time.'

In a minute or two she was back, giggling. 'He's got a brother of his comin' out on the bus with him next Friday night to help bring in Agnes her water.'

I couldn't understand why that made her so happy. 'If I was grown-up I wouldn't let Agnes have any water,' I said. 'Not ever. Not even to drink.'

'That's 'cause you're dumber than dumb,' Cathy said. 'His brother comin' out means we'll have comp'ny. Comp'ny means Agnes can't go gettin' all mean and smiley on us. Comp'ny means we'll get to eat!'

Cathy was right. Friday we cooked all day and by the end of it, all our heads were covered with lumps and bruises from the butt-end of knives, pots and pans, and the rolling pin. But then the man we were to call Uncle Larry walked in with the Old Man and we got to sit down and eat!

Studying Uncle Larry across the table gave us a good idea of what the Old Man might have looked like a long time ago. Uncle Larry's face was ruddy, his hair thick, and he didn't wear glasses. He laughed a lot and talked to Agnes the way we one day dreamed of talking to her ourselves. He made her spitting mad was what he did and the madder she got, the harder he laughed and the more we liked him.

'You sure got a fine-looking bunch of kids workin' for you, Agnes,' he began, pointing with his knife at Cathy. ''specially that 'un. Reg'lar beauty, she is. Makes me wish I'd had me a girl.'

'A tomcat like you with a kid?' Agnes spat. 'Humph! More'n likely it'd end up like this bunch, homeless trash.'

'Yeah, but homeless trash sure pays good, don't it, Agnes?' Uncle Larry countered. 'Bet your mattress is all over lumps with what-all you got hid away inside of it, huh?'

I came bolt upright in my chair at those words. It was money making that mattress all over lumps? I'd always wondered. But ... how could he know that?

The other kids, forks halfway to their mouths, waited for Agnes to explode at him for saying such a thing but she just turned so red her eyes watered while Uncle Larry rocked with noisy laughter. Holding her gaze firmly with his own, as though more than anything he'd like to see her try and stop him, he picked up the serving dishes and piled more food on our plates than we'd ever had at one sitting.

Agnes didn't say a word about the food, but she got back at him saying, 'What you tryin' to do, huh, Larry? Turn 'em into hogs like your own self?'

Uncle Larry looked around the table at us, his eyebrows raised in mock dismay. 'You hear what she done called me?' he spluttered. 'Me? Lovable Larry? A hog ain't exactly what my lady friends call me, Agnes,' he preened. 'My lady friends call me—'

But Agnes didn't want to know what his lady friends called him. Instead she was on her feet, slamming her chair under the table, saying, 'What I need to know, Larry, is did you come out here to eat and talk, or dig me a well?'

Uncle Larry's eyebrows went up again. 'You better start talking prettier than that to ol' Lovable Larry, Agnes, else there ain't gonna be no diggin' and no water and what's your Betty gonna say about that?' He rocked with laughter at the expression that came on her face at the mention of Betty. A look of both disbelief and anger.

'Oh, yeah!' he spluttered, his tongue and fingers meanwhile working at particles of food wedged between his teeth. 'Been meaning to tell you 'bout me'n Betty having us real nice long chats three or four nights a week. The way she tells it, I'm your last chance at running water, Agnes. Says neither her nor none of them boys of yours is coming near so long as you keep filling the place up with homeless trash and don't put in running water. So how 'bout that, Agnes?'

Agnes tossed her head. 'I guess nobody got around to tellin' you the armed services ain't givin' out weekend passes like before.'

Uncle Larry gasped in mock amazement. 'Is that right? Then I guess I better have me a talk with the Pres-i-dent ask him how come I got to have two of yours at my place just this past weekend? You s'pose they was AWOL?'

Agnes bit her lip and spun away to the stove where she took out her humiliation on the pots and pans.

Laughing uproariously Uncle Larry slapped the Old Man on the shoulder, 'Let's get to it then, boy, long's I'm here!' he said. He shook his head and sighed, 'Still can't figure how come I let myself get talked into comin' out. Sooner I'm back in town, happier I'm gonna be.'

He turned to the boys, 'Want you guys out there, too, hear? Gonna need all the help we can get.'

The hole they started digging was right outside the kitchen and our bedroom was above the kitchen. As darkness fell the men strung up a light bulb that reflected on our ceiling and it was comforting for us to lie in bed listening to Uncle Larry and the boys talking and laughing. In the darkness, Agnes sat on the edge of the bed watching the work going on down below. Her weight made the bed tip so badly I had to cling to the edge of my side of the mattress with all my fingers to keep from rolling into her but I comforted myself knowing that, if I did let go and Agnes yelled and hit me, all I had to do was call for Uncle Larry and he would come up and rescue me.

And Saturday morning there was further comfort knowing Agnes couldn't get started on her usual, spiteful routines at the chicken table. Not with the men digging close by, she couldn't.

After lunch Agnes amazed us by doing something Cathy had always sworn she never would: all decked out in her pink Knitting-Bee dress and her hair combed, she set out to catch the bus to town and deliver the chickens herself.

As she trudged away through the woods carrying her heavy load, the sun, as if by magic, seemed to shine in a kindlier manner, a breeze stirred the trees, and the men took time to lean on their shovels and kid with the boys.

Moving away from the hole they'd been digging they headed for the barn – us kids in chattering, giggling pursuit – where they broke open a crate that had been there ever since James and I arrived. Inside was a little machine they said was a pump. They carried it into the kitchen and nailed it to a wooden stand they'd built on the floor next to the sink. Late in the afternoon when Agnes returned and saw it she actually laughed out loud. Hugging herself with glee she said, 'Never thought I'd see the day I'd have me runnin' water right here in my own kitchen!'

At supper, Uncle Larry said, 'Nothing comes up out the ordinary, Agnes, we'll get your water hooked up tomorrow.' He looked around the table. 'Guess you won't be needin' so many kids to run the place then, huh? What say I take a couple of these here girls back to town, put 'em to work for me, huh? What say, girls?'

All three of us girls stopped chewing at the enormity of what he'd just said. Would he really take us? But wait. He said a couple. That meant one of us would get left behind.

'Big a fool as Bennings is,' Agnes glowered, cutting short our rising hopes, 'she ain't that dumb.'

Uncle Larry laughed – he must have thought it funny to tease little kids – and turned to the Old Man. 'What say you and me get duded up and raise a little hell tonight, old guy? Saturday night don't come round but once a week.'

Instantly Agnes whirled away from the range to stare down on the Old Man. 'You ain't going no place, Walter!' she growled. 'You got that?'

To Uncle Larry she spoke in a whiney kind of way. 'Larry,' she began, swaying her shoulders and acting like a bashful little kid, 'You said – you promised, even – you was gonna bring me in my water. You go out raising hell tonight, you'll be sleeping all day tomorrow.'

144

Uncle Larry chuckled, 'I was just putting you on, Agnes.' Sticking a toothpick between his teeth, tilting back in his chair, he looked her up and down slowly before adding, 'Reckon I know as well as the next guy there ain't no real women hereabouts anyways, Agnes. Figure I'd just as soon get finished up here quick so's I can get back to town find me a whole bunch of cuties.'

Sunday morning the hole outside the kitchen window was so deep the only way you could tell the digging was still in progress was by the shovels full of dirt flying out of it. Yet even with all six of us kids carrying the dirt away in buckets as fast as we could, there was still a mountain of it waiting to be moved.

Late morning the dirt unexpectedly stopped coming out of the hole and the men, covered head to toe in dirt and sweat, came out instead. They sat down on the porch steps.

Agnes stormed through the screen door. 'How come you're settin'?' she wanted to know, 'You done?'

'You tell her, Larry,' the Old Man said.

Uncle Larry laughed his big loud laugh, 'Looks like old Wally here done got his numbers wrong, Agnes. We done run out of pipe.'

Agnes gasped, 'You settin' there tellin' me I ain't gettin' my water today? Is that what

145

you're tellin' me?'

'That's what I'm settin' here tellin' you, Agnes, you ain't gettin' your water,' Uncle Larry said. 'Leastways not this week, you ain't.' Agnes started screaming she had to have her water. Today! She said, 'I talked to Betty on the telephone last night and she said she might could come out next weekend if'n there was water so what am I supposed to tell her now, huh? That her old man and her uncle can't do nothing right? That all I got to show for a weekend of cooking and aggravation is a hole in the ground and a pile of dirt?'

Uncle Larry yelled right back at her to shut up and mind her tongue. 'I'll call Betty tonight when I get back in town and tell her what happened,' he roared. 'Meantime get back in that kitchen of yours fix some food for me'n Wally and these kids else by God I'll put you in that hole and pile that dirt in on top of you.'

Agnes had no choice but to fix food for Uncle Larry and the Old Man but 'the kids ain't got time to eat,' she glowered. 'They got to get out haulin'. Get water on them vegetables else how'm I supposed to feed 'em come winter?'

'Suit yourself,' Larry said, and then he was holding his sides laughing, 'Look at it this way, Agnes, you get to have me back next weekend. You ever think you'd get that lucky?'

146

Uncle Larry and the Old Man finished their lunch and went to sit on the porch of the cabin. They put their feet up on the porch rail and a bottle of whisky passed back and forth between them. We saw them every time we staggered by with a bucket of water.

Danny came up with an idea. 'Cathy,' he said, 'on account of Uncle Larry liking you best, go ask him for a quarter so one of us can run to the store real quick get us each a candy bar.'

Cathy shook her head, 'Uh-uh. Not me. What if Agnes calls us in and I'm not here? I might could miss supper as well as lunch. I ain't askin' Uncle Larry for nothin'.'

We began working on a different strategy to approach the men but just then Uncle Larry stood up and called and waved for us all to come over to the cabin porch.

Did he have candy? Money? What...?

He waited till we were all lined up in front of him before sitting himself sideways on the porch rail, one foot swinging.

'Me'n your daddy has had us a idea,' he began. 'Gonna give you all a treat. Gonna have us a game of hide and seek with candy bars for the winners! What say? Sound like fun?'

He winked, looked over at the house, put his finger to his lips, 'Gets us all away from old you-know-who, don't it?'

147

'Yeah!' we chorused. 'Sure does! Let's go!'

All of us except Cathy. Flat out, she said, 'We can't. Agnes ... Mother ... she'll be real mad if we quit haulin'.'

'Ha! She gets mad, I'll get madder!' Uncle Larry said, standing up and thumping his chest. 'OK, go on now and hide. Boys go one way, girls t'other. Me'n your Daddy's gonna count to one hundred real slow give you time to get far, far away!'

Dropping their buckets right where they were, the boys ran towards the barn. I saw Cathy look over at the house and knew she was going to hide close by in case Agnes did call. Well, I wouldn't! I didn't care if Agnes beat me. I wanted a candy bar so bad I'd begun to drool. It didn't look as though Sally was going anywhere so I called out to her to come with me. 'I know a real good place down by the well where there's that nice big clump of pine trees we can hide under,' I said.

It was cool in our hiding place and nice to let the dried-up pine needles slide through our hot, sweaty fingers. We heard the men's calling voices fade away in the distance and Sally giggled. She had such a lovely giggle, Sally, one that was almost never heard. She said, 'It's gonna take 'em a while to find us here!'

That worried me. 'Maybe we shoulda hid some place closer,' I said. 'I'm hungry! I got to get that candy bar pretty darn quick. And I'm gonna ask Uncle Larry to write a letter to my folks to come get me away from this terrible, awful place.'

'Me, too,' Sally said, her eyes lighting up. 'Only I'm gonna ask if I can go live with him on account of he said he liked girls and I sure like him!'

'Yeah,' I said, 'I like him, too, only ... only I wish he'd just given us the candy and not made us stop haulin' to hide. Agnes'll be worse'n ever after he leaves.'

Sally's eyes widened. 'Yeah ...' she whimpered. 'And tomorrow's Monday. We gotta do the wash...' She yawned and rubbed her eyes even as a tear leaked out.

'You can't go to sleep,' I warned. 'If they don't find us real soon we'll have to go find them!'

'I ain't,' Sally mumbled, and slept.

Now what was I supposed to do? I couldn't leave her there, could I? But if I stayed we might never get found and then we wouldn't get any candy bars and more than likely, no supper either. Wait! What was that noise? I turned around and here came Uncle Larry pushing his way through the low-hanging branches. I was so happy to see him my mouth started watering again and I couldn't even talk. All I could do was smile and smile.

He flopped down beside me. 'You girls sure give me a run around, I swear!' he panted. 'I been lookin' everywhere! What's this? Sally's sleepin'?'

'I told her not to!' I said. 'I'll wake her up now. She wants her candy bar and we want to ask you–'

Uncle Larry grabbed my hand before it touched Sally. 'Leave her be!' he said. 'I need to rest a spell. I'm all wore out diggin' that damn well and chasin' you girls all over hell and gone.'

He slid closer to me and stretched out and ... all of a sudden he didn't seem so nice. Close up I could see his dirt-encrusted face, his bloodshot eyes, the sweat streaming down into the stubble on his chin and it seemed odd to me that a grown-up man would get that hot and out of breath chasing after a couple of little kids.

He smelled, too! Worse even than the Old Man because his whisky breath mingled with the stink of his sweat.

I wanted to move away but what if he got mad? Uncle Larry propped himself up on one elbow and looked around. 'You girls sure found yourselves a dandy hidin' place right here,' he grinned. 'Nobody'd find you 'less they was lookin' real hard.'

He reached out and put his hand inside the bib of my overalls and I didn't like that. Grown-ups weren't supposed to put their hands inside kids' clothes, were they?

'Reckon you got a mite of growing to do

up here yet, ain't you child?' he said. 'How old did Agnes tell me you was?'

'I'm going on seven,' I lied, leaning away.

'Hey!' he frowned. 'Don't go pullin' away from your Uncle Larry like that! Come on now, move back close and give me a nice big kiss.'

Ugh! I didn't want to give him a kiss. I leaned away further still but he grabbed me by the shoulders with both hands and pulled me close and forced his tongue between my teeth. His stubble scratched my face and his whisky-drool filled my mouth and it was the most disgusting thing that had ever happened to me.

I struggled to get away but he held me tighter yet with one hand while the other went down between my legs inside my overalls and his fingers – those filthy, mud-caked fingers – were poking inside of me and it hurt and I fought even harder to get away.

Uncle Larry groaned and, struggling to his knees, took both my hands in one of his and held them tight while his other hand unbuttoned his fly. His trousers fell down around his knees and he was holding his thing – a big red one – in his other hand. 'Bet you ain't never seen one this big before, huh?' he laughed. 'What they call these here in England?' he asked.

I didn't know. Didn't even know if men in England kept big, ugly things like that in their trousers. All I'd ever seen before was James' and it was small and white.

Uncle Larry arched his back and thrust towards my face so all I could see were his dirty fingers with the black fingernails clutching himself. 'Kiss it!' he panted.

I turned my head away as far as it would go and saw that Sally was awake. 'Make him stop!' I gasped. Sally didn't move. 'Go get James then,' I pleaded. And still Sally didn't move, just blinked and yawned, and somehow, to me, that seemed the worst part of the whole situation – that Sally wouldn't help me.

'I said kiss it,' Uncle Larry growled. 'I'm ready, boy... You want a candy bar, don't you?'

I was so scared I was choking and crying and struggling all at the same time and I couldn't answer but I shook my head ferociously, meaning, 'No! I won't kiss it. Not even for a candy bar. I won't! Let me go!'

Uncle Larry took one of my hands and put it underneath his so we were both gripping his penis and his hold on my hand was so tight it hurt. Soon he was panting and twisting and moving back and forth ever faster while some kind of sticky looking wet came spurting out of him.

After what seemed like forever, the panting and the shaking and the wetting stopped. Uncle Larry let go of my hand and flopped down beside me. Quickly, I plunged my hand deep in the pine needles to get rid of the feel of him and started inching away on my backside.

Uncle Larry grabbed my ankle, 'Stay put!' he ordered, looking at me in a sad kind of way and shaking his head as though I'd done something really, really bad.

'You was supposed to kiss me and make me feel good,' he sighed. 'Damn me, but I shoulda listened to Wally back there and gone after that Cathy. She knows what to do! Or even that one,' he looked at Sally. 'Wally says she does it real good even if she ain't but a baby.' He looked thoughtful. 'You know what?' he said. 'I've a mind to tell Agnes on you, that's what.'

Getting to his feet he pulled me up beside him and leaned down till his face was close to mine. 'You gonna do like I say next time or am I gonna have to have me a talk with Agnes?' he asked.

I didn't know what he meant or what he was going to tell Agnes or what it was Cathy and Sally did that I should have done.

Uncle Larry leaned in closer yet so his breath was hot against my face and I reeled from the stink of it. 'I'm gonna go back now,' he said. 'Gonna say I never did find neither one of you. But come next week,' he wagged his finger, 'and you carry on like you just done, I'm tellin'!'

Backing away he disappeared in the branches and I sat down abruptly. Not because I wanted to but because my shaking legs couldn't hold me up any longer.

'Get up right now,' Sally said in an unusually firm voice for her. 'We got to go back else we won't get no supper like we din't get no lunch.'

I told her I wasn't going back because he'd be there and I didn't want to see him again. Not ever. I said, 'He's not nice like we thought. He's ugly and he stinks and he does things he's not supposed to do and he touched me where he's not supposed to touch me. I hate him!'

'So what?' Sally said. 'I got to eat. You'd have done like he said we'd both be eatin' candy bars right now.'

'I bet you wouldn't have kissed that ugly, disgusting thing,' I moaned.

'I would, too! Nights you go knittin' it's what me and Cathy does to the Old Man else he won't give us our Milky Way bars.'

I didn't understand any of it. Couldn't think why the Old Man and Uncle Larry would want them to do that or why Sally didn't seem to care.

'How come they do that?' I began, 'Why...?'

'Me'n Cathy can't figure it neither,' Sally shrugged. 'Just ... they like it, I guess. Come on.'

My legs still didn't want to hold me up.

Sally said, 'You don't get a move on right now Agnes might could send Uncle Larry out lookin' for you!'

Gasping, I scrambled to my knees and Sally pulled me up the rest of the way.

There were empty chairs at the supper table when we crept in – the boys' chairs – and not a word was being spoken by anyone. There was only the sound of knives and forks scraping across plates to break the silence until Agnes spoke, saying, 'If them boys can't move their backsides for supper they ain't getting none. Dump 'em in the hog slops, Cathy.'

I cringed inwardly knowing how much the boys needed those suppers while wondering if the men had even gone looking for them. Were they still hiding? Or had they been given candy bars and told to stay away?

Sitting in my place at the table, I couldn't get my eyes up off my plate to look at anyone except Cathy. But Cathy wouldn't look back. She wasn't even watching Agnes' face as she usually did. Instead her head was low over her plate and I saw that when she tried to put food in her mouth it took her a while because the hand holding her fork was shaking.

I knew then it didn't matter what Sally or Uncle Larry said about Cathy being good at whatever it was she did to the Old Man, because right then Cathy was very, very

155

upset. So upset she was fighting herself not to cry.

And there was something else I knew, too. I knew it wasn't worth a candy bar. No, not even ten candy bars. Maybe not even a hundred...

NINE

In the days following Uncle Larry's visit it seemed to me he was still there, so filled – crammed – was my head with images of him: slouched across the table, eating like a pig, on the cabin porch, digging in the hole and, most particularly, in the hiding place by the well. My ears, too, still rang with his coarse, jeering laughter and his taunting remarks. In the odd times he was absent from my thoughts, my mind occupied itself with what I had learned about the Old Man and I lived in mortal fear that Agnes would carry out her threat of not taking me to the next Knitting Bee so that I, too, would be called upon to go downstairs and kiss him.

'The way you been actin' these last days, girl,' Agnes repeatedly warned, 'fallin' over stuff and breakin' stuff and forgettin' what-all you're supposed to be doin', ain't no tellin' what you might could do to disgrace me I take you knittin' this next time.'

She was right. In spite of my good intentions, I no sooner began a chore than my head filled up with what to do if I didn't go to Knitting and the Old Man called me down.

From there my mind raced ahead to Uncle Larry coming back and what he was going to make me do or what he'd tell Agnes I didn't do and next thing I knew, Agnes would be coming at me, madder than a bull, fists flailing, wanting to know what in hell had gotten into me.

I almost did tell her the first time she asked. I almost said, 'Uncle Larry's what's gotten into me, ma'am. He's a bad, disgusting man and can I please stay in the house with you next time he comes?'

I didn't, though, because I'd already learned through my own experience, and from listening to Cathy, one of the most unfair and frightening lessons of childhood: it didn't matter how badly adults behaved or what they said or did to you, other adults always took their side. 'It's your own fault,' they'd say, all tight-lipped. 'You only have yourself to blame. You must have deserved it or it wouldn't have happened.'

The one person I most wanted to talk to was Cathy. But Cathy wouldn't let me. One night when we were saying the rosary I tried yet again, whispering under the drone of Hail

Marys, but she only hissed at me to shut up and prayed extra loud.

Anyway, Cathy's bed-wetting, once a rare event, had worsened to the point she was wetting every night and she was getting into plenty of trouble on account of it.

'I didn't know better,' Agnes fumed, watching with disgust as Cathy pulled the sheets off her bed and hung them over the window ledge to dry, 'I'd take you for a spoiled Limey brat like Sarah 'stead of the good American kid you're s'posed to be.'

Agnes stood by her threat not to take me with her to the Knitting Bee up to the moment she herself was almost ready to leave the house before she relented. 'I don't,' she complained, 'I'll have all them old biddies traipsin' up to my front door wastin' my time wantin' to know if the poor darlin' refugee kid is doin' all right and bringin' you stuff. Go get changed.'

If it hadn't been for knowing what the Old Man was doing to Cathy and Sally back at the house, I might have wished Agnes had left me behind because the whole way there she raged about what dumb, ugly, lazy, spoiled Limey brats James and I were. On the way home, the Royal Family, Winston Churchill and all the British armed services were added to her grievances and, knowing there was no longer any danger of anyone seeing telltale bruises and lumps on my face

158

and body, accompanied her remarks with vicious slaps, pinches, and thumps.

In spite of my many fervent prayers and feverish plans to run away if he came back, Friday night brought Uncle Larry once again to the supper table. I could not get my eyes up off my plate to look at him. Not even when he asked Agnes, 'How about the Limey? She been doin' what-all you told her this week?'

'She's been drivin' me crazy all week, is what she's been doin',' Agnes glowered. 'Haven't got a lick of work out of her the whole entire time. Kid's done everythin' I told her ass-backwards.'

Uncle Larry turned to me, 'What about it, girl? You gonna start doin' what-all you're told right from here on in?'

Before I could get my voice around the ever-present lump in my throat, Agnes answered for me. 'She don't straighten out right quick,' she snarled, 'she's going back where she come from, never mind the bombs and what-all.'

My heart leapt. Oh, if only she would! Send me back to the bombs and what-all! After her, and then Uncle Larry, Adolf Hitler himself seemed like a dear, kindly old friend. What could I do to make her?

'You oughta do that, Agnes,' Uncle Larry agreed. 'I'm serious. Get rid of her, get you a nice American orphan kid like Cathy in her place.' He chewed thoughtfully a moment before adding, 'You could get yourself in a heap of trouble taking in kids that's got folks of their own, see. Even if'n they're thousand of miles away and a war goin' on.'

'Mind your business, Larry!' Agnes snapped. And to us girls, 'Get this kitchen cleaned up and get on up to bed. These men has better things to do than talk to a bunch of no-count brats while I'm still waitin' on my water.'

An odd thing happened once the men and the boys were back outside digging with the light shining up on the ceiling again. I felt better than I had the whole week worrying about Uncle Larry coming back because I knew he couldn't come up and get me. Not with Agnes sitting on the side of the bed looking down on him, he couldn't.

Reasoning further, I realized – figured – he'd be down in that hole the next day, too, and maybe ... maybe they'd finish up sooner than they thought – the pipe they'd ordered had been delivered during the week – and they'd go off raising hell like he also said last week.

The irony of this situation didn't strike me until years later when James and I began looking back: that inasmuch as Uncle Larry and Agnes were the two people I feared and hated most in the world, I nonetheless looked to each as a protector, one against the other, when necessary.

It was Uncle Larry's raucous voice we heard calling us from our various chores late the following Sunday morning.

When we got to the kitchen he was standing with his back to the sink, his arms stretched wide like a magician who'd just performed an amazing trick. He bowed us forward, then stepped aside pointing dramatically to the water pouring out of the tap into the sink. With another grand flourish he directed our attention to the little pump on the floor, its fan belt whirring so fast all we could see was a blur.

Our eyes went wide. 'No more haulin',' Danny breathed.

'That's right, boy, no more haulin'!' Uncle Larry crowed. 'Step up here, Agnes, show 'em all how it works. Turn it off.'

Letting go of her bottom lip and shaking her head as if she couldn't believe the wonder of running water, Agnes stepped forward, reached out and turned the tap. The water flow stopped instantly and the little pump on the floor went silent, its fan belt still. 'It's like a miracle,' she gloated. 'I got me water!'

'Give me a kiss for it then, Agnes,' Uncle Larry demanded. 'You owe me a kiss!'

Ugh! Those men and their kisses!

Agnes turned a dark and indignant red but she leaned forward and pecked Uncle Larry's ruddy cheek so quickly it was as if she thought her lips might catch fire on his face.

'That ain't no kiss,' Uncle Larry howled and before Agnes could step back he'd pulled her close with his hands on her backside and his mouth on hers. What was he doing? Why was he bending her over backwards like that? And why would he want to kiss her anyway? Did he have his tongue in her mouth like he did with us? Oh, they were so disgusting!

Abruptly, Uncle Larry let go of Agnes and she nearly went down backwards in her efforts to keep her balance. 'Don't know how you ever got it on with her, Wally,' he complained, wiping his mouth with the back of his hand, 'You can have her and welcome.'

In the silence that followed, we felt both shame and disgust for the three adults standing before us. Kids though we may have been, we knew that Uncle Larry did not have the right to kiss his brother's wife the way he had. And yet, the Old Man seemed unconcerned, merely turning away to look out the window as though nothing unusual had happened, while Uncle Larry, grinning, hitching up his pants, looked at us as if he'd done something really smart and expected our approval. Only Agnes, head bowed, fists clenched, face so red and angry it looked as if it might disintegrate at any moment, showed her feelings.

The silence lengthened, the adults remaining as they were, motionless, as though all three were actors in a play and had forgotten what came next. At the same time, we all became aware of a new sound, a sound none of us recognized at first – the sound of water dripping from a tap.

At any other time we kids might have wondered about it, or at least been curious, but right then we had other things to think about. Scarcely breathing we were waiting to see if Agnes or the Old Man were going to do anything about the way Uncle Larry had just behaved. Would either one hit him? Cuss him out? Tell him to git?

They did nothing! Turning, pointing, Agnes vented on the boys instead. 'Git!' she ordered, 'You seen water before, ain't you? And you girls! Get some food going! Jesus Christ, do I have to think of everythin'?'

Our contempt and loathing for her went up another notch. She was a coward and now we wished Uncle Larry would grab her backside and bend her over backwards again. Serve the bitch right.

Uncle Larry agreed with Agnes. 'Yeah, kids,' he urged. 'Hurry it up. We got stuff to do this afternoon. Important stuff!'

Agnes didn't eat lunch that day. Didn't

even sit at the table, but stood, on guard, as it were, beside the sink, one hand on the tap, as if protecting it from unseen enemies.

Uncle Larry took a long swallow from the whisky bottle he and the Old Man were passing back and forth between them, and said, 'It ain't gonna go away, Agnes. I do somethin', I do it right!'

He got to his feet, 'Gonna take these kids offa your hands for a while now, Agnes, have us some fun,' he winked at me. 'Got some new games lined up reckon even the Limey'll want to play along.'

'Ain't no games gettin' played around here till these girls has cleaned up and washed these dishes,' Agnes said. 'Get to 'em, girls. And mind yourselves around my pump. Anybody busts it, their head gets busted.'

As soon as we had the kitchen to ourselves, I whispered to Cathy, 'Let's just keep doin' these dishes over and over till supper time. They might could forget their dumb games.'

'They ain't gonna forget their games,' Cathy moaned.

'Then I ain't goin' out there!' I said. 'I'll do something so bad Agnes'll have to tie me up. I know! I'll hit her. Right in the face!'

'Won't do you no good,' Cathy said. 'You seen for yourself she's scared to death of him–'

She broke off as a shower of water hit her full in the face. She whirled on Sally, 'Quit that!' she hissed. 'Quit messin' with her water!'

Sally giggled and kept right on doing what she was doing: pressing her finger tight up against the tap so that the running water sprayed in all directions.

Cathy grabbed her hand, twisted it away from the tap, slapped it and said, 'I told you quit it! Now clean up this floor 'fore Agnes sees what you done!'

'Look!' I gasped. 'She even got water on the pump!' and I flicked at the drops with the dish towel I had in my hand. Without warning, the towel was whipped out of my hand by the speed of the fan belt and I was toppling forward onto the pump. The fan belt stopped whirring, the water stopped running, and in the silence that followed all three of us stared, dumbfounded, at the dish towel caught up in the fan belt, and at the great drops of blood splashing and spreading in the water on the floor.

'Oh, Jesus,' Cathy moaned. 'You done busted her pump. And look at the mess you're makin'. Quick! Get rags! We got to clean up!'

I was out the door while she was still talking and racing towards the grapevines where the mop and floor rags were hung to dry. Dimly I was aware that the men on the cabin porch could see me but I didn't care. I'd busted Agnes' pump and we had to fix it before Agnes fixed me. Maybe forever.

Heart racing, I grabbed up the mop with one hand and a handful of rags with the other. Instantly the rags were soaked with blood and I remember wondering if all that blood could be coming from me? But if it was, so what? I just wrapped the rags around my hand and raced back to the kitchen where Cathy was holding the screen door open with her foot, both hands held out to take the mop and the rags. I was almost there when I heard running feet and saw the Old Man and Uncle Larry approaching from the cabin.

'Gimme the rags,' Cathy gasped, grabbing for them. The rags came off my hand just as the Old Man came alongside.

'Oh, shit!' he groaned, 'Take a look at that, will you. She done took the top offa her finger.'

I had? Sure enough, through the spurting blood the top of one of my fingers could be seen dangling by a slender thread of skin.

'Must've got it caught in the fan belt along with that dish towel,' Uncle Larry conjectured.

Agnes crashed in from her office, took in the wet, bloody floor, the dish towel caught in the belt of the silent pump, the blood running down my arm and dripping off my elbow, and started screaming, 'She busted my pump! Years I waited on it and that goddam Limey bitch has gone and busted it!'

Grabbing the mop from my other hand she started flailing. Her blows were meant for me but everyone was getting hit, even the men, all of us ducking and trying to get out of her way. Uncle Larry grabbed Agnes' arm and wrestled the mop away from her. 'Get a-hold of yourself, woman,' he roared. 'Kid's hurt bad enough as it is.'

'The kid?' Agnes screamed. 'The kid? What about my pump?'

'There a doctor hereabouts?' Uncle Larry asked.

'Down by the store a-ways,' the Old Man said, grabbing up a dish towel, wrapping it around my bleeding hand and steering me towards the door.

Agnes blocked our way, arms outstretched, screaming, 'She ain't seein' no doctor. I ain't spendin' good money on a doctor when it's her busted my pump. Who's gonna pay to fix that?'

To me their voices seemed to be coming from far away and I sagged against the door frame to keep myself from falling. Feeling was coming back into my finger and I was in an agony of pain.

Dimly, I saw Uncle Larry grab hold of Agnes, push her into her rocker and hold her there, his hands pressing down on her shoulders. 'You-all go on,' he called. 'I'll be right behind you.'

The Old Man picked me up and I noticed

James hovering by the door looking white and scared. 'Can he come with us?' I pleaded, my voice little more than a whisper.

'Why not?' the Old Man said. 'Be one less kid for her to beat up on.'

The next thing I remember was being in a little white room where an old man with white hair that matched the walls of the room was stitching my finger back together. That, and the sound of my own screaming. The Old Man was holding one side of me and Uncle Larry the other and through the prisms of my tears I could see James crouched in a corner on the floor with his eyes tight shut and his fingers in his ears.

An old lady was there, too. A kindly old lady. She was handing the doctor the things he needed and talking to me.

'There, there, honey,' she soothed. 'Nearly done. There, there.'

When the doctor snipped the thread with the scissors she handed him, she said, 'There! See! What did I tell you? Doctor Healey's finished and guess what? You've still got your whole entire finger! Hold still now while I get you bandaged up.'

Uncle Larry dropped my arm and stepped back saying, 'Lord God almighty, girl! Never heard such a racket in all my born days. Thought you Limeys was supposed to be tough.'

Doctor Healey told him finger injuries

were very painful. 'Nerve endings, you know...' Turning to me, he asked, 'And what's a little English girl like you doing way out here?'

I was still too busy gulping and sobbing to be able to answer and Doctor Healey was too busy turning my head this way and that, fingering the multitude of cuts and bruises put there by Agnes, to notice. 'Looks like you make a habit of running into things, doesn't it, child?' he said. 'Head. Arms. Legs.' He turned to the Old Man, 'She a relative?'

'It's the wife,' the Old Man muttered, 'The wife takes in foster kids.'

'Ah-ha!' Doctor Healey said, as though that explained everything. Turning to me he said my finger was going to be good as new. 'Come back Friday,' he said, 'so I can take a look-see. Maybe take some of these stitches out.' He looked at the lady, 'Maybe Mrs Healey will fix us some tea and cake that day,' he suggested, 'and we'll have time for a nice long visit.'

'Absolutely,' Mrs Healey beamed. 'Tea and cake it will be. And bring this brother of yours along with you.'

Walking back to the house, Uncle Larry told the Old Man that Agnes was plumb crazy. 'I was you I'd get the hell out of there,' he said. 'Fast!'

'I can handle her,' the Old Man said.

'Yeah, I noticed,' Uncle Larry sneered. 'You handle her real good, Wally.'

The Old Man was so dumb he took that as a compliment and smiled.

'Me, I'm leaving just as soon's we get back,' Uncle Larry went on. 'Couldn't sleep knowing she's running loose around the place. 'Sides, ain't got nothing to stay for,' he scowled at me. 'Ain't gonna have us no fun like we planned the way things has turned out. Jesus! And I worked my ass off two entire weekends on that damn well of yours.'

Just as he said those words, we came out of the woods and Uncle Larry stopped walking and let out a low whistle. 'What's she got going on there, Wally?' he asked, nodding towards the porch.

James and I could have told him what she'd got going on. What was going on was one of Agnes' favourite tortures. The one where she made kids kneel on the splintering planks of the porch, their hands tied tightly to the roof supports with rough twine. As a finishing touch, a rag filled with either soap, vinegar, or pepper was always added as a gag to each howling mouth.

Uncle Larry ran the rest of the way to the house with James and me close on his heels. Yanking open the screen door he strode into the office and confronted Agnes, gently rocking in her rocker, wearing her 'smiley' smile.

'You can go to jail for that, woman,' Uncle

Larry roared, jerking his thumb towards the porch.

Her eyes riveted on James and me, Agnes acted as though she neither saw nor heard him. Her slow, soft smile widening she spoke to us, saying, 'I been waitin' on you. Seems like we got some accounts to settle, don't it? My animals ain't had a drop of water this whole entire day on account of you bustin' my pump. And my vegetables is out there wiltin' ... dyin'... Go get haulin'. We'll talk more when you get done.'

'Yes, ma'am,' we mumbled, backing away.

Uncle Larry stopped us with his hands on our shoulders and turned on Agnes. 'Your fuckin' pump ain't busted, Agnes,' he roared, 'though I've a mind to go bust it right now. Shit, even a fool crazy as you oughta be able to figure that one out.'

Striding to the pump, he disentangled the dish towel, set the belt back on its runner and turned the tap. Water gushed forth. 'That look like it's busted?' he sneered.

He walked to where he was looking down on Agnes again. 'And another thing,' he said, his hand on my shoulder, 'this kid ain't doin' no chores. The doc back there give her somethin' so's she can sleep through the pain and that's what she's gonna do, Agnes, sleep.' He pushed me towards the stairs.

Mounting them I heard Uncle Larry yell at Agnes to untie the kids on the porch else he'd have the cops out, but I felt so sleepy so warm ... I didn't hear what Agnes said back. Besides, I couldn't remember why ... what ... I was supposed to be doing up there. I lay down on the bed to try and figure it out.

TEN

Out of nowhere, it seemed, Cathy was beside me, hissing in my ear, shaking me, dragging me off the bed. 'You gotta get a move on ... get downstairs. Agnes has gone crazy-mad. Been screamin' and yellin' all mornin' long. Poured boilin' water on Sally's hands 'cause she was washin' slow and, boy, wait'll you see the blisters...'

I couldn't make any sense out of what she was saying. My head felt so fuzzy and my mouth so dry I couldn't think at all. Cathy pulled me harder and I rolled over on my hand and instantly I remembered everything. The pump! The blood! My finger! Uncle Larry! Oh, Jesus! Oh, God!

'He gone?' I gasped, 'Uncle Larry?'

'Left yesterday,' Cathy answered and paused a moment to smile. 'Took time to give Agnes a black eye 'fore he left though!'

Oh, how I wished I'd seen him do that! And oh, how I wished he was still there to keep Agnes away from me.

'What you s'pose she'll do to me now?' I gulped.

Cathy looked as scared as I felt. 'Whatever it is, it ain't gonna be nice,' she said, pushing me towards the stairs.

From the bottom step I could see Agnes at the wash tub and quickly slid my bandaged hand behind my back. Agnes turned and saw me. 'Hope you're feelin' rested bein' all you done since yes't'day is sleep,' she growled.

'Yes, ma'am.'

'Hope you ain't 'spectin' no breakfast.'

'No, ma'am.'

'What's that you got behind your back?'

'Um ... my hand, ma'am.'

'Your hand, huh? Bring it here. I been wantin' to have me a look-see. Cathy, go get me my scissors.'

Scissors? 'No!' I gasped, backing away. 'Please, Mother...'

'I ain't your mother,' Agnes snarled. 'I was you'd be dead! It's on account of you my own kids don't come near! On account of you I had that pig, Larry, beatin' up on me yesterday! Get over here!'

I struggled as hard as I could but she got my hand out from behind my back and slammed it down on the table. Cathy handed her the scissors, then gave all her attention to the floor. Agnes cut the bandage away, tugging where dried blood had

173

stuck it to my skin.

'Why ... this ain't nothin' but a itty-bitty scratch,' she glowered staring at my discoloured, grossly swollen finger. 'And that old fool put in four stitches? Jesus! Must think my name's Rockefeller! Cathy, honey, let's us take 'em out! Leastways, two. Go get me them little pointy scissors out of Betty's room.'

More scissors? Little pointy scissors? While desperately trying to tug my hand free of Agnes' vice-like grip, I begged her to leave them alone. 'Please, ma'am...' I sobbed. 'They already hurt real bad and the doctor said he'd maybe take a couple out Friday.'

'You ain't goin' no place Friday, girl,' Agnes snarled. 'What? Pay that old fool extra when if I'd had my say I'd have just lopped the top of that finger right off. For free, too! Damn them interferin' men!'

Over the racket of my screams and sobs, Agnes, frowning and squinting and complaining loudly at how tightly they were swollen in, picked and poked at the stitches with the points of the scissors, causing fresh blood to spurt and twice the pain the doctor had when he originally put them in.

'Damn your noise,' Agnes said at the last, shoving me aside. 'Get out of here. Don't want to see your face, hear that ugly voice no more today. Git!'

Once outside, blinded by tears and racked

with sobs, I blundered forward intent only on putting as much distance between myself and Agnes as I could. I came to a confused halt at the sound of my name being called.

Squinting through my tears I looked around but saw no one. There it was again, 'Sarah!' and still I could not locate its source. On the off-chance it was my guardian angel, I looked heavenwards even though I knew in my heart that guardian angels were one more thing Mummy had been quite wrong about. If they were real, wouldn't mine have kept me from falling on the pump yesterday? And would it have let Agnes beat me up and pull my stitches out just now? Come to think of it, why had it let James and me come to this frightening, dangerous place to live when, if it was doing its job, it could just as easily have found us a nice little home like the ones across from Bill's store?

And that was just my angel. What about James' angel? If mine was busy, his could have helped, couldn't it?

Again I heard the voice, 'Sarah!' and that time I saw an arm waving from behind the barn.

All three boys were back there and I let out a little chuckle when I saw they were smoking. Next to candy, cigarettes were a favourite item with all us kids although we only got hold of them when the Old Man passed out. Without being asked, James reached out and

175

let me have a puff of his.

'We didn't get but the three,' he explained when I asked for one of my own, 'on account of leaving him one in the pack...' His voice trailed off and his eyes widened as he noticed my uncovered, hugely swollen, purple, black and blue finger still leaking blood. Wordlessly he pointed it out to Danny and Andy.

Cringing at the sight, Danny felt enough pity for me to let me have a puff of his cigarette and then, albeit reluctantly, Andy did the same.

Danny said, 'Cigarettes wasn't the only thing we got ahold of last night when the Old Man passed out. Take a guess at what else.'

'A quarter?' I ventured.

Barely able to restrain his mocking laughter, Danny said, 'How about ten bucks?'

'Ten bucks! I don't believe you.'

'It's true!' James said. 'And we're going to use it to run away!'

'Yeah!' Danny said. 'She's not beatin' up on us no more!' He pointed to an angry-looking black and blue welt running along his left jaw bone. 'That's where she got me with the mop handle yesterday. Right there!'

Andy, who rarely spoke, held out his arms and legs for me to look at and I saw dark, angry red welts all over them. 'An' we never even done nothin'!' he muttered.

For a brief moment I stopped feeling sick and hungry and scared. 'Let's leave right now,' I said. 'We could get far, far away!'

'You're not goin',' James said quickly. 'This is just us guys. Soon's we get jobs and a place to stay, we'll come back in the night and hide in the woods till we can sneak in and rescue you girls.'

'That's not fair,' I gasped. 'Us girls has to go now, too, else she'll make us do all your work and I'm scared of the hogs and that crazy Suzy cow. And if I don't do everything just right she'll hit me. Right on my finger. You know she will.'

The boys stared at me and they stared at my finger and James said, 'She's right. We got to wait till her finger gets better.'

Just then I remembered something I had been told long ago and I said, 'Remember, James, how Mummy used to say if ever we were in trouble or needed help to look for a policeman? If you went and found one and told him how wicked and cruel Agnes is, I bet he'd come right out and take us all away at the one time.'

Danny rolled over backwards laughing at me. 'I can't get over you're that dumb,' he chortled. 'Nuts as well. Cops is grown-ups. We go talk to them alls they'll do is bring us right back. Tell us we don't know when we're well off!'

Andy startled us by speaking again, 'Ain't nobody bringin' me back, boy! They try, I'll jump out the car. I'm goin' tonight.'

'No, you ain't,' Danny said. 'You're stayin' put. We go, we go together.'

Just then the bell at the house rang for lunch and the boys took off running. James stopped and called back to me to hurry. I answered saying I couldn't. I said, 'Agnes said she didn't want to see my face no more today.'

'Come with me,' James said. 'I'll take care of you!'

Yeah, sure. If he could take care of me we wouldn't even be here, would we? I went with him anyway, partly because I was too hungry to stay behind, and partly because I thought Cathy or Sally might have done something to make Agnes mad at them and she'd have forgotten about my ugly face.

Something, indeed, must have happened because the Agnes sitting at the table was talking excitedly and didn't even notice me, while my only thought was to eat my sandwich as fast as I could before she snatched it away and threw it in the hog slops.

Swallowing the last bite and once more able to pay attention to what was going on I saw that Agnes was glaring at Danny and I guessed she must have asked him a question he didn't know how to answer. Cathy cleared her throat. Danny blinked and smiled a big, fake smile.

'What's the matter with you, boy?' Agnes asked. 'You've heard of a birthday party before, ain't you?'

Danny made his smile go wider, 'A birthday party!' he exclaimed. 'For me? Gee! Wow!'

Agnes' smile came back and everyone giggled with relief. Agnes pushed her chair back from the table saying, 'You girls clear up this table. Me'n the boys are gonna go get started building us a bar-be-cue like this here one I found,' she waved a picture torn from a magazine. 'Sally, run on down to the store pick up what I already called in.'

Alone in the kitchen with Cathy, I voiced my misgivings, 'It don't seem natural for Agnes to be doin' somethin' fun and nice for a change. It ain't like her.' I paused to let out a sigh. 'Not but what she won't still beat us up. Anyway, I figure I already missed my birthday this year, but if they're fun and nice like they are in England I could pretend like I didn't and maybe get one, too.'

Cathy looked worried. 'We all got birthdays comin' or goin' and ain't none of us dumb enough to talk about 'em. Not till we see what-all happens at Danny's. How're we supposed to know how to act, huh?'

'In England,' I began, 'you play games and get presents and a cake and you get to blow out the candles on your cake and make a wish and everyone sings Happy Birthday to you.'

'This ain't England, remember?' Cathy

said with a roll of her eyes. 'Shut up till we see...'

Under the trees in the orchard, Agnes and the boys were putting together a kind of low, square wall with some old bricks. Nearby, the door we used to pluck and gut the Saturday chickens on had been turned over on its stand to its clean side. Sally was standing next to it, her arms protectively cradling a package of hot dogs, a package of buns and a bag of marshmallows.

Cathy and I stared in disbelief. We were going to get to eat all that food? When we just ate lunch? Could Agnes be in a good mood?

Agnes was holding up the picture from the magazine for the boys to look at. 'Look at it good,' she urged. 'Stack them bricks right and leave spaces in between 'em like it shows. If it works like it's supposed to we'll cement the bricks together next time we got left-over cement from makin' another path.'

Following Cathy's lead, Sally and I tried to find the correct stance for a barbecue birthday party. Hands behind our backs or arms folded in front? Behind our backs felt best.

We tried out different faces. Frowning and serious? Smiling and happy? How about surprised? As if watching Agnes and the boys was really surprising? Nah...We looked down at the ground and that felt safest.

'We're going to light the fire now,' Agnes

announced. We faked big, excited smiles and moved forward. Agnes handed a packet of matches to Danny. 'Bein' you're the birthday boy,' she said, 'you get to light the fire.'

Even though Danny's hands were trembling a little from all the unaccustomed attention he was getting, he managed to strike a match. He touched it to the paper and twigs but it went out. 'You got to blow on it, dammit,' Agnes growled.

Danny struck a second match, touched it to the paper and blew and blew. A puff of smoke appeared but no flames.

'Give me them matches!' Agnes growled, 'Jesus Christ! How come I have to do every damn thing around here?' She stepped forward quickly, lost her balance and would have fallen heavily if Danny hadn't grabbed her by the elbow and steadied her.

Pushing her glasses back up her nose, Agnes smiled down lovingly on Danny. 'How come you just tried to trip me, boy?' she purred.

Danny turned white. 'I ... I never tried to trip you, ma'am,' he stammered. 'Soon's I saw you stumble, I–'

Agnes grabbed his arm, twisted it behind his back, told him to quit lying. She turned to the rest of us. 'You seen him stick his foot out same as me, ain't that right?'

We looked everywhere but at Danny as we mumbled, 'Yes, ma'am.'

Agnes said, 'Come to think of it, there ain't gonna be no party for Danny today. I tried and he done made a fool out of me. What we're gonna do is eat his share while he's doin' all the chores on his lonesome, bein'...' her eyebrows went up and she tossed her head, 'we're gonna be otherwise engaged.'

Danny looked so awfully little limping away in his too-big overalls, his protruding arms and ankles thin as sticks, the back of his neck and his ears a dark red, it was hard for us girls to keep from crying, but Agnes thought he looked funny. 'Ha, ha!' she laughed before calling after him, 'We're gonna sing a birthday song for you, Danny boy! Oh, yeah! We're gonna have us a real fine party and just so's you won't feel lonesome we're gonna sing, "Danny has to work while we have us a party!"'

She turned to us, 'Sing!' she ordered. 'You heard me. You know the words. Sing!' Grabbing up a stick, she thumped a cadence with it on the chicken table and started singing herself, 'Danny has to work while we have us a party...'

While we sang, I prayed. 'Dear God, never mind the hot dogs and the marshmallows, just please don't let her ever think about giving me a party. Thank you. Amen.'

Agnes had a fine time at the party. When it was over, she said, 'I just wisht I'd had me a camera so's I could've took a picture, mailed it on to Bennings. Like that she coulda seen for herself the fine kind of life I'm givin' you no-count kids.'

Sitting slumped at the breakfast table next morning, as though throwing a birthday party had sapped her of all her strength, Agnes, with a deep sigh, announced we were going to can tomatoes that day. Her lower lip trembled. Reaching for the hem of her dress, she patted away tears from beneath her glasses.

'Wasn't for you-all I wouldn't need to,' she sniffed. 'Wasn't for you-all I'd be settin' in a nice little house in town with every modern convenience buyin' me one tomato at a time whenever I felt like eatin' one. Wouldn't have acres of the damn things waitin' on me.'

Again she pulled up the hem of her dress and dabbed away tears. 'All this I do for you,' she sighed, 'and what do I get back, huh? Trouble and cuts and sores and doctor bills and that fool Larry beatin' up on me is what I get back.'

She got up from her chair and told the boys to get on out, start picking. 'These girls'll be out just as soon as the Old Man here gets done messin' up my kitchen and wastin' my time with his godamm shavin' over the sink like he does every damn day.'

No sooner had the Old Man shuffled out of our way, than we raced to get through the dishes and out of the house. Agnes crying and complaining at the breakfast table was bad enough. But Agnes sitting quiet in her office, not even rocking, was worse.

Out in the field we found three bushel baskets half full of tomatoes but no sign of the boys. Cathy aimed a vicious kick at one of the baskets. 'Them boys is so dumb!' she scowled. 'They'll get us all killed talkin' and foolin' around and her actin' the way she is. You two start in pickin' while I go find the dumb jerks.'

As always, we followed Agnes' rule of starting at opposite ends of a row, Sally and I, the idea being we wouldn't waste time gabbin'. We were nearly met in the middle before Cathy came back, panting for breath. 'They ain't here!' she gasped. 'I been everywhere lookin'. Even went to the store. They's gone. Runned away!'

Sally jumped up howling, 'You're lyin'!'

That's what I thought, too, because they said they'd wait till my finger got better. 'How do you know?' I asked.

'I just told you!' Cathy spluttered. 'I been everywhere. And when I looked in the cabin I seen all their stuff's gone. Shoes. Clothes. Everythin'.' Her eyes went small and mean. 'Dumb jerks ain't gonna get far. Too little! Too dumb! First grown-up sees 'em, they're back.'

Sally turned and started running towards

the house howling that she wanted her brother. Cathy grabbed her and turned her around. 'Shut up and start pickin',' she ordered. 'Let Agnes find out her own self like we done. We need to give the dumb jerks time to get good and far.'

We picked for a long time always expecting Agnes to come out checking on us but she never did.

Finally the bell rang for lunch. 'Mind now...' Cathy warned as we headed for the house. 'We don't know nothin'. Just we ain't seen 'em.'

Agnes wasn't in the kitchen or her office when we crept in so we ate our sandwiches standing up and wiped our plates on our backsides so we wouldn't have to wash them. We gulped water right from the tap so we wouldn't have to wash our glasses and just then Agnes walked in, saw the boys weren't there, hadn't eaten, and demanded to know where they was at.

'...Uh ... we ... um ... don't know, ma'am,' we mumbled, all together.

'Cathy, go find 'em, tell 'em to get their backsides in here on the double.'

Cathy was out the door before Agnes finished speaking. Sally and I, thinking we had to pick more, headed for the door only to have Agnes stop us, saying, 'You two get on over to the sink start in washin' them tomatoes you already brung in.'

While we worked we could hear Cathy's calling voice, sometimes near the house and at other times so far away we could barely make it out. Meantime, Agnes paced the kitchen, back and forth, side to side, slamming the table with the strap she was carrying every time she passed it by.

She pulled up in front of me, 'When was the last time you seen 'em?'

'At breakfast, ma'am.'

'How about you?' she asked Sally.

'Same's her,' Sally whispered.

'You telling me them bastids ain't done a lick of work this whole entire day?' she shrieked. Spinning away from us she nearly collided with Cathy coming in the door. 'Well?' she demanded. 'Well?'

Panting, Cathy said, 'Couldn't find 'em nowheres, ma'am.'

Agnes slashed all three of us out the door with the strap. 'Git!' she roared. 'Go pick!'

Back among the tomatoes we kept our heads low but we knew exactly where Agnes was every second. She went to the cabin last and, after only a brief interval, came out at a lumbering trot.

'She's got it figured now, boy,' Cathy sighed.

We kept on picking while we wondered, sometimes out loud and sometimes in whispers, what the boys were doing and what Agnes was doing. Then, unexpectedly, we heard a car coming up the dirt road. The last car to come our way had been old Bennings delivering James and me.

Forgetting what Agnes would do to us if we stopped work, we ran to the back of the cabin to see who it could be.

The dust was so thick that for a time we couldn't make out anything but then Cathy gasped, 'Jesus! She done called the cops!'

She had! Two cops were climbing over the fence and walking up to the front door.

'They did like I said,' I rejoiced. 'Found a cop! They're here to take us away!' and started running towards the house.

Cathy pulled me back by my overall straps. 'You don't know that for sure,' she said. 'Could be she called 'em.'

'Lemme go,' I panted. 'You're wrong. I told 'em to find a cop. That's how come they're here!'

'Danny's way too smart to go looking for a cop,' Cathy said. 'And if a cop found him he'd lie and you better, too, they start in askin' questions. Lie, else shut up! Right now we need to get back pickin'. Act like we don't know what's goin' on.'

Cathy and I had picked a full bushel basket apiece and topped off Sally's before the bell summoned us to the house. Sally started to sniffle and Cathy told her to quit it. She said, 'We ain't even s'posed to know how come them cops is here so what you got to cry

187

over, huh? And remember, you don't know nothin'.'

To my puzzled eyes the kitchen, when we entered it, seemed to be much smaller than usual. I wondered how that could be until I realized – figured out – that big cops in uniforms sprawled either side of the table, legs stretched out full length, sideways, take up a lot of room.

From her place, standing at the head of the table, Agnes said, 'Officers, these here's the sisters I been tellin' you about.'

The officers set aside the framed photographs they had in their hands and we recognized them as the ones from the top of the piano in the parlour, the ones showing Agnes' four kids wearing their dress uniforms. It was obvious from the way the cops were looking from the pictures to Agnes they thought she was one fine, upstanding woman. They thought her kids were pretty fine, too.

Head slightly bowed, Agnes smiled her Virgin Mary smile and said, 'Girls, these officers is here on account of it looks like as if your brothers has done run off. These men are going to help find 'em before... Oh, Officers...' she stifled a sob, 'I'll never get over it somethin' bad happens to them boys.'

Her hands went around our shoulders and she pushed us forward. The officers didn't notice that her nails were digging into our sun-burned skin. 'These officers just want to ask you a couple questions,' she told us, 'and then you can run back out and make more mud pies.'

Head to one side, she eyed our dusty overalls, our dirt-caked hands and feet, smiled the long-suffering Virgin Mary smile again and said, 'I just can't keep them out the dirt no matter how hard I try.'

One of the cops, the older, fatter one, sat up straighter and asked, 'Any of you girls ever hear your brothers talk about running off?'

Like a trained choir, we chorused, 'No, sir.'

'Know if they had any money?'

'No, sir.'

'Know any reason why they'd run off?'

'No-o-o-o, sir.'

'When was the last time you seen 'em?'

'At breakfast, sir.'

'Anything out the ordinary happen yesterday could have made 'em want to skip?'

'Um... No-o-o-o, sir.'

'Nothing at all?'

'No, sir.'

Agnes interrupted. 'Like I said before, Officers, it's got to be the British boy's doin'. Has to have been. He's bigger'n the others and what you might could call a ring leader. Ain't had nothin' but trouble since he come, though mind, the girl's a perfect little lady.

Knits and all.'

The old cop nodded as if he understood. 'Sounds like you got yourself a bad apple, ma'am. Young pup didn't know when he was well off. Well ... like they say, boys will be boys and lordy don't I know it! Got three my own self and they give me fits.'

He stood up. 'You don't have a thing in the world to worry about, ma'am. Me'n my partner'll find 'em, have 'em back in no time at all.'

The younger cop patted Agnes on the shoulder. 'Could be you're too easy on 'em, ma'am. It was me, I'd give 'em a good strapping just as soon's they come through the door. Meantime, just rest easy and leave it to us, ma'am. We don't find nothing right away, we'll be back out first thing in the morning with the dogs.'

Both men smiled down on us girls and the old, fat one said, 'Be extra good to your momma, hear? She's got a lot on her mind right now with her own fine kids far from home and them young hoodlums running off like they done. Enough to try the patience of a saint.'

Agnes showed the cops out the front door and on her return we could tell she was pleased with herself by the way she crossed directly to stand in front of the Old Man's shaving mirror, patting her hair and giving herself big smiles.

'I guess them fine brothers of yours never give a thought to you-all havin' to do their chores when they skipped, huh?' she began, turning away from the mirror. 'Start in with the milkin' and don't come cryin' to me about Suzy actin' up. Don't want to hear it. Just get her milked.'

In the barn Cathy said, 'Sally, go collect eggs. You can leave the ones where the hens are settin' on their nests. Me'n Sarah'll come get 'em later. Sarah, on account of your bad finger you milk Clara and I'll milk mean old Suzy and just let the dumb thing try something on me!' She started milking.

I began to suspect then that Suzy understood people talk because right after Cathy said that, she rolled her eyes so the whites showed, backed up and knocked Cathy and the bucket over. Milk went everywhere.

Enraged, Cathy jumped up and kicked Suzy in the belly as hard as she could. 'That's what you get kickin' over your bucket,' she hollered. She turned to me. 'See! That's how you got to treat her. Mean. It's easy! Just act like it's Agnes and it's downright fun!'

I jumped up from my milking stool and aimed a kick at Suzy, saying, 'You bet I will! I'll show her!'

Right away Suzy bunched up again and kicked out at both of us, sending us crashing into the opposite wall and that's when I knew for certain Suzy understood people talk.

Cathy got to her feet first, and while she was rubbing her head and her arms and her back and trying not to cry, said, 'I swear! Bein' little and bein' a kid's got to be the two worst things can happen to a body.'

I was surprised it had taken her so long to figure that one out. After all, she was nearly nine and I already knew it when I was just a little kid still living in England.

ELEVEN

We were just finishing our cornflakes the next morning when the cops showed up, hardly able to restrain two big, panting, slobbering dogs. Agnes, who had been on her feet pacing and cussing, awaiting their arrival, saw them coming up the path and hollered, 'I ain't having them animals trackin' dirt through my parlour! Bring 'em round back.'

The Old Man was still at the table when Agnes let them in. He sat for a long moment scratching his head and clearing his throat and shuffling his feet under the table before saying, 'I got a couple things I got to say to you guys. Private.'

On an indrawn breath, Agnes drew herself up tall. 'Anything you got to say to them I need to know. I'm the one responsible. I'm the one has to talk to Bennings and them others in town.'

The Old Man sighed, bowing to the inevitable. 'Well then, I counted up my cash yesterday and I'm ten bucks short.'

Agnes, fists clenched, eyes narrowed, glared at him as though she'd like to rip his head off his shoulders and shred it.

The Old Man pushed back from the table and picked up his lunch box. 'That's all I got to say,' he muttered and headed out the door so fast he forgot to shave.

Huddled together by the window, the cops reasoned out the new situation between them: 'Them boys having money puts a whole new light on things. With money, they could've paid to take the bus to town. Maybe even gone so far as the railway station and bought themselves tickets to God only knows where. We need to check that out...'

Drawing apart, one of them turned to Agnes, 'Ma'am ... long as we're here might just as well let the dogs have theirselves a sniff around, see where their noses take 'em.'

Agnes nodded her assent and went to sit in her rocker but she didn't rock and she didn't go through her picture box, just sat staring out the window in the direction the cops had taken, her fingers busy with her lower lip.

Finished with the dishes, we didn't know if we were supposed to wash the tomatoes we'd brought in the day before or go pick more so we stood in the shadows, still and quiet as statues, ready to go either way. The phone rang and Agnes got up to answer it. She said 'No' a lot of times and 'Yes' a few, then hung up with a bang and came into the kitchen.

'Them cops must've talked around 'cause one of them busybodies from Knittin' has got word of this and is wantin' to know if I need comp'ny,' she said. 'Someone to share my grief … my heartache.'

'Grief?' she spat. 'Heartache? Only thing grievin' me right now is my achin' back and work. Work them boys ain't doin'. Work you ain't doin'. Get busy now, wash up them tomatoes. It's you-all's gonna put 'em up. I need to set.'

She pulled the rocker to where she could watch us – supervise, she called it – and told us to get going.

I didn't need to look at Cathy to know what she was thinking. She was thinking the same thing I was: we were too small to put anything up by ourselves. Even standing on the stool, we couldn't reach to stir to the bottom of the big, tall pot Agnes used for canning. And when the tomatoes finished simmering and were ready to go into jars – we carried spoonfuls to Agnes so she could see for herself – there was no way we could pick up that pot and pour. Agnes told us to figure it out ourselves and we tried but, even together, the

194

pot was too heavy and too hot and we spilled more on the table than we got in the jars.

The cops were still there and we could hear the dogs woofing and whining, so we knew Agnes was just waiting. Waiting and watching, toes tapping, to make us pay for the waste. In particular, she had her eye on Sally and when the cops left she was the one who was going to get it first. Oh, boy, was she ever.

Sally hadn't stopped crying for Andy since he left and because of the usual hair hanging in her face – hair Agnes always refused to pin up or tie back saying, 'Why would I bein' I can't stand the sight of her ugly face?' – couldn't see what she was doing so all she'd done all morning was drop things and knock things over.

She'd already broken two jars and cut herself picking up the pieces. More ominous for her, though, was the fact that she was fidgeting and pressing her knees together, which meant, as Agnes well knew, that she was desperate to go pee.

The cops knocked on the door. Agnes couldn't very well let them in, could she? Not with us girls doing the work of grown women when she wanted them to think we were outside making mud pies. She went outside instead. There was some talk, loud 'Goodbyes' and 'Take cares', and then Agnes was back inside holding the boys' overalls.

'Them cop dogs found these here stuffed in

that old hollow tree down past the hog pens,' she said. 'Do you beat that? The three of 'em out there in the woods changin' into their Sunday finest and then headin' off to the bus stop – that's where the dogs was pointin' – with my money in their pockets and my tomatoes layin' out there dyin' on the vine.

'I hope they have a right good time to theirselves,' she went on, ''cause time they get back here I'll have figured ways to fix 'em ain't nobody even dreamed about yet.'

Sally hiccupped on her sobs, moaned, and a puddle spread around her feet.

Agnes' eyes lit up. The time for revenge had come. Her lips pulled back from her teeth in a savage grin. 'Always said you wasn't nothing but a animal,' she exulted, 'Time now for me to treat you like one!'

Grabbing Sally by her overall straps and the seat of her pants, she carried her, face down and screaming, outside.

Not caring that if Agnes were to look our way, we'd be next, Cathy and I ran to the screen door to see what she was going to do with Sally.

She carried her to a place in the yard where she had the barn straight ahead of her, the chicken house to one side, the hog pens on the other and there she hesitated, as if she couldn't make up her mind where to dump her.

Watching her, it wasn't hard to figure out

196

how her brain was working. She took a step towards the hog pens. Weren't they the dirtiest, smelliest of the animals? And wasn't that what she always said Sally was, a hog?

But we could see her arms were tiring and Sally was getting heavier by the minute with all her screaming and kicking and the hog pens had a high fence she'd have to lift her over. She turned towards the barn. It was closer, but wait ... the cows weren't there. The Old Man had staked them out earlier so what was the use?

How about the chicken house, then? It was close and the door was wide open. Yeah, that would do it! After manoeuvring her noisy burden through the wire gate to the run, Agnes approached the house, threw Sally in, then slammed the door and bolted it shut on the outside.

Cathy moaned, 'That there's got to be the meanest damn thing Agnes ever did. Good and well she knows Sally's scared to death of them chickens.'

We scurried back to the table and tried to pour more tomatoes into the jars before Agnes came back. But we soon realized that the pot and its contents, off the stove, had cooled somewhat while we were looking out the door and we knew it would be easier to just scoop up the tomatoes with our bare hands and cram them in the jars.

By the time we heard Agnes on the path

outside, the pot was light enough to lift and tilt and, grinning at our inventiveness, we filled the remaining jars.

Even though it was so hot outside that the grass had turned brown and crunched when we walked on it, it was cooler than in the kitchen and Cathy and I were so happy to be outside and away from Agnes and her cruel fists, we were practically dancing.

We'd finished 'canning' – a term that always mystified me since glass jars were used, not cans – and were on our way to bring the cows in for milking.

'Milkin' Suzy's gonna be downright fun after bein' around Agnes the live long day!' Cathy giggled.

First, though, we had to let Sally out of the hen house. We entered the run and Cathy slid back the bolt on the door and we both yelled at Sally to come on out and get busy pickin'. Hot, stinking air hit us in the face and we reeled backwards.

'Je-sus!' Cathy gasped. 'It's hotter in there than the inside of Agnes' oven. Get on out here, Sally.'

Sally didn't answer and she didn't come out. Cathy took a deep breath, pinched her nostrils closed and stuck her head inside.

'Jesus! Will you look at that!' she exclaimed. 'She's layin' face down sleepin' on top of all that chicken shit. Maybe Agnes is right. Maybe she ain't but a animal.' Louder, she said, 'Wake up, Sally. You got to get pickin'.'

Sally didn't even lift her head and after we yelled some more, alternating dire threats with unrealistic promises of candy, and she still hadn't budged, Cathy said, 'Looks like we're gonna have to go in and haul her out.'

It took us a while to get ourselves in a position where we could get hold of her, a leg each, and pull because as Cathy said, 'That door was made for chickens, not people, and we ain't goin' in there, no sir. Too hot! Stinks too bad!'

We got Sally out a leg at a time, an arm at a time, then the rest of her, but we couldn't make her stand up. Maybe she couldn't? She was limp and damp, her face had a greenish tinge to it, even her lips, and her eyes were closed. Head to toe she was caked in chicken droppings and feathers.

'Sally you got to stand up!' Cathy hollered, trying to shake her by her limp shoulders. 'You got to clean yourself up! You stink! And you need to get pickin'.'

Sally's head lolled from side to side with the shaking, her mouth hung slack, and it was hard to tell if she even heard.

'She ain't actin' right,' Cathy said. 'Agnes sees her like this, she'll … dunno. Ain't much more she can do, is there? We got to clean her up.'

'We can't!' I gasped. 'Agnes is waitin' on the milk.'

'Let's just get her in the barn then. Look! Her tongue's hangin' out! Shut your mouth, Sally!'

We thought she might need a drink of water but where to get her one? Couldn't go in the house... Well was too far... We remembered the cows had water in their buckets and if they hadn't knocked them over – the dumb things did that all the time – we'd give her some of that, even if it would be boiling hot.

We pulled Sally's limp body into the barn and sat her down leaning against the wall and tried to get her to drink some cow water by cupping it in our hands. Sally wouldn't, or couldn't, swallow any at all and, seething with frustration, not knowing what else to do, we gave up on her and had just started to milk when we heard Agnes coming our way.

Leaping to her feet, Cathy said, 'C'mon. We got to squat down in front of Sally so's Agnes won't start in on her again.'

'She'll start in on us if we ain't milkin', though,' I argued, but did what Cathy said, like always.

Agnes was too happy to notice anything. 'Them nice police officers just called!' she preened. 'They found them lyin', thievin' brothers of yours not a mile from the bus station in town eatin' ice cream! I'll give 'em ice cream!' she snarled. 'That's my money they was eatin'! They slep' in a park last night!' she went on. 'I'll give 'em sleepin' in a park in their good clothes. Time I get done with them they ain't gonna be able to sleep no place.

'I told them nice officers, bein' it's late in the day to just go on ahead and keep 'em overnight, give 'em a taste of jail... Bring 'em out in the mornin'.'

She looked directly at me then and her smile widened. 'All 'ceptin' that no-good Limey brother of yours!' she jeered. 'I told 'em, "Him, I ain't fixin' on takin' back. No, sir! He's the one started all this – stealin' my money ... leadin' them others astray." I called Bennings on the telephone just now and she said the same on account of she knows there never was any kind of trouble out here before he come.'

She stopped smiling and leaned towards me. 'Know what a reform school is, girl?'

'No, ma'am.'

'Same thing as a jail!' Agnes rejoiced. 'A jail for real bad kids! It ain't just me, see. Ain't a family in the state wants a thief in the house. They tried every place.'

She looked at me as though expecting me to cry. Or look ashamed. Or at least beg her to please, please let him come back. But I was too happy to give her the satisfaction of either my tears or my pleas. I was glad he wasn't coming back. It meant he could tell people what a cruel, wicked woman Agnes was and if they didn't believe him, he'd just have to find a way to come and rescue me. He had to. It was, after all, his job.

We were sent out to pick tomatoes again first thing next morning, but we didn't. Instead, we squatted down behind the cabin watching and waiting for the police car that was bringing Danny and Andy back.

The cabin perched a little higher than the dirt road so it was easy to look down on it. We saw the car's dust over the treetops long before the car itself rounded the last bend and came into view. By the time it stopped at the fence there was such a cloud of it we could hardly see it at all but we heard the motor stop and doors slamming. As the dust slowly settled we were able to make out Danny and Andy and just one cop making their way, single file, to the front door.

They were filthy dirty, those boys, and walked in an odd, limping kind of way. 'Look at that, will you,' Cathy muttered. 'Betcha the dumb jerks ain't wearing socks. Must've forgot 'em. Don't you just know they've got big, bloody blisters all over their feet?'

Agnes opened the door and we heard the cop say something, her say something back, and then the cop turned and went back to his car and drove away.

Agnes must have gone to watch from an upstairs window because the moment the cop's dust trail got as far away as you could see from the house was the moment the screams started. Awful screams. Heart-breaking screams. Worse than anything we'd ever heard before. So awful we clung to one another trembling and flinching as if we were the ones being whipped.

After a while, a long, long while, the screams stopped, the back door opened, and the boys were thrown out bodily. Their shirts hung in ribbons and their faces and upper bodies were slick with blood. Like some grotesque species of deformed humanity, they lay where they landed. Cathy stopped her whimpering and got mad instead. 'I told 'em,' she said. 'Only way out of here is to shut up and grow up. Maybe now they'll listen when I tell 'em stuff.'

I said I wasn't staying till I grew up! 'James got away and I will, too!' I said, 'Even if the stupid war goes on forever and ever.'

Sally hadn't said a word since we pulled her out of the chicken house the day before, just sat staring blank-eyed at nothing, her mouth open and drooling, but she agreed with us then. At least we thought she did. She nodded her head.

'That just goes to show you're both still babies,' Cathy sneered.

'Call me anything you want,' I said. 'It don't

make me no never mind 'cause I'm going to think up something real, real bad to do so I'll get sent away to reform school like James.'

'You might just as soon think up something real good to do on account of Agnes don't know the difference no more,' Cathy said.

I opened my mouth to say something back but nothing came out because I suddenly knew Cathy was right. Agnes didn't know the difference. And that was just about the scariest thing I ever had to think about and I hated Miss Know-it-all-Cathy for making me think it.

TWELVE

With James, from this point on, no longer a part of the Slater household, and each of us having led divergent lives ever since, I expected him to lose all interest in our long-overdue quest for joint memories and veer off into lengthy descriptions of his life elsewhere, something about which I had always been curious and anxious to hear.

But this didn't happen. Instead he insisted on hearing every remaining detail of all that had transpired at the Slater home after his departure, so I had no choice but to keep on going.

I told him that once I knew he was safe in a reform school, and thinking my own troubles would quickly come to an end through his expected intercession, I spent as much time as I dared hanging around the various paths in the woods, expecting that at any moment he would appear on one of them and smuggle me away to a wonderful new life.

Once Cathy figured out what I was up to and why, she put a swift end to it, saying, 'Don't you get it? He's in jail. A kids' jail! That means he's locked up, dummy. And you oughta know by now there ain't a grown-up alive that'll believe a word he tells 'em. Alls they'll do is call him a liar. That's how come you got to keep your own mouth shut and lie when you have to.'

As if to back up Cathy's position, a letter for Agnes arrived from my father, the first he had ever written, having previously preferred to leave such matters to my mother. There were a lot of big words in that letter that no one, least of all Agnes, understood, but the gist of it was that he was deeply saddened and shocked by his son's behaviour and it was fortunate for James they were not on the same continent and there was a war in progress because otherwise, rest assured, the punishment for what he had done would be swift and severe. Meanwhile, he begged Mr and Mrs Slater to accept his most sincere apologies and his assurances that, as soon as this terrible war ended, full restitution would be made.

That letter was sweeter than a love letter to Agnes. After reading it to the Old Man and us kids so many times we knew it by heart, she called Bennings and, as if the woman barely understood English, read it very slowly and deliberately to her. Finally, she carried it down to the store and read it to Bill.

'Too bad your dad didn't send her a halo to go along with that letter,' Cathy sneered. 'That way everybody'd get to see her the way she sees herself – like some kind of a saint. You know, good old Saint Agnes.'

With Daddy's betrayal as final proof, I took Cathy's advice and stopped looking for James.

And now at last, Agnes was satisfied by the new, silent behaviour of all us kids. 'Whoever it was said spare the rod and spoil the child must've been some sharp cookie,' she commented, ''cause take a look at what one good lickin' and that hen house done to you all.

'It maybe took me awhile,' she went on, 'but now I got you acting the way foster kids that're lucky to have a roof over their heads is supposed to act, with never a word out of none of you and no time wasted lollygaggin' around. 'Bout time, too, with school starting up in a couple weeks' time, Godammit!'

206

'School?' I questioned Cathy the first time I caught her alone after Agnes' announcement. 'She actually lets us go to school?'

'There you go again with your dumb questions,' Cathy groaned. ''Course she lets us go to school. She flat out has to. There's laws about it.'

'You mean she ain't figured a way to trick the folks that make the laws?'

'Not yet, she ain't.'

Still I could not believe it. Whole days away from Agnes instead of just a few minutes a week when our turns came around to go to the store? 'But...' I persisted, 'who's gonna do all the chores while we're at school?'

'Take a guess.'

Agnes spelled it out so I didn't have to. 'Don't think for one minute I'm lettin' you all sneak off to school and leave me with all the work,' she announced one night at supper. 'No, sir-ee! Didn't sign up for all the trouble of you, the work, the worry, to get stuck doin' the chores, as well. And seein' how it's comin' soon, might as well get caught up on what-all I got in mind right now.'

She had a lot in mind. She started all five of us in the vegetable field where, under the blistering sun, we picked or dug up every vegetable still out there. From there she moved us to the orchard where we stripped the trees of all their fruit, ripe or not.

Then it was into the suffocating, steam-fogged kitchen for us girls where, for over a week, the harvest was canned and hauled away to the cellar.

With field and orchard stripped bare, Agnes moved us to the woods where she had the boys, using the chicken axe, cut down dead trees and the girls haul them to the saw horse back of the barn where the boys sawed them into logs.

They had to be very careful to cut the logs to Agnes' exact specifications, those boys, or, as Cathy warned, 'Count on her going after you with that axe, maybe lopping off a couple of your fingers while she's at it.'

Agnes wanted the logs small enough to fit easily through the opening on the top of the range, but not so small they'd burn too fast.

'Why don't you go tell her bring us out a ruler,' Danny sneered to Cathy, 'and some chalk to mark 'em?'

'I had a ruler, I'd break it,' Cathy said. 'And if you ever get hold of one, you better too, else have her beatin' you upside the head with it.'

'She don't need no ruler for that,' Danny said, fingering the lumps on his head. 'She's doing just fine with the logs.'

When the logs were all the right size it fell to Cathy, Sally and me to stack them in rows, one on top of the other, alongside all the outbuildings as high as we could reach.

'How come we got to stack 'em out here?'

I asked Cathy, pulling splinters out of my scratched and bleeding hands and forearms. 'Why not nearer the house?'

'So's they won't blow down we get a big storm ... come winter.'

'How can logs blow down when the trees already done that?'

'Not the logs, dumbo! The buildin's!'

After supper was cleared away the night before school started, Agnes said, 'Want you girls upstairs trying on them raggedy old clothes Sarah brought with her from England. Need to see what-all does for who.'

I pulled on the first dress Agnes handed me.

'You done outgrowed it,' she said. 'Give it to Cathy.'

The second one went to Sally, then another to Cathy, then Sally again. When we got down to the last one, the frilly one I wore to Knitting Bee, I tried to trick Agnes. 'Look!' I exclaimed. 'It still fits! I can wear it!'

She shook her head, 'You done outgrowed that one, too. Give it to Cathy.'

'Oh, but... Please let me keep it, else–'

Agnes stood firm. 'Ain't nothing worse to look at than a great big girl like you with her backside hanging down b'neath her skirt. Give it to Cathy and count yourself lucky I thought to hold on to them dresses I made up for my Betty back when she was a kid,

209

else you'd be going to school naked, girl.'

Pulling down a cardboard box from the top of the hall closet, Agnes dumped it out on the bed. Everything in it smelled musty and disgusting. Digging around in the pile, she pulled out two faded plaid dresses with deep sweat stains under the arms. 'Try 'em on,' she ordered.

I took a deep breath and silently prayed, 'Please God, don't let 'em fit.' I tried them on and they didn't! Thank you, God! The skirts of both came down to my ankles and the short sleeves to my wrists. Nobody, not even Agnes, could say they fit.

'Look at that, will you,' Agnes marvelled. 'They fit like they was made for you! Take 'em downstairs, now, iron 'em up. Take your shoes down, too.'

The boys were already sitting on the bench in the kitchen, their shoes lined up in front of them.

'Put 'em on, Godammit!' Agnes growled. 'You didn't bring 'em over to look at, did you?'

It's never easy getting hot, sweaty feet into shoes that have dried out and curled up over the summer, especially without socks, so it took us a while with Agnes pacing and fuming and swinging the strap in our direction the whole time.

When at last we stood before her, she said, 'Godammit! You done outgrowed 'em! Jesus!

Cathy give yours to Sally and wipe her slobbering mouth. Sarah give yours to Cathy. Danny give yours to Sarah. Andy you keep yours and don't nobody go telling me they hurt. There ain't no money for new ones. Not with me a kid short, there ain't.'

'Please, ma'am ...' I faltered, made desperate by revulsion at the sight of Danny's scuffed and misshapen shoes, 'Really and truly and honest to God, my own fit better'n Danny's, look.'

'Do you think you're the Queen of England?' Agnes exploded. 'Or one of them princesses? You'll wear what I tell you else what's Cathy supposed to wear? Danny you wear that old pair of James'. Too bad he run off in his good 'uns.'

Moonlight still flooded the bedroom when Agnes shook us awake for the first day of school. 'Strip them beds and get the wash goin',' she ordered. 'And while you're at it strip Betty's bed, too, on account of from now I'm gonna be sleepin' in there on my ownsome. Ain't fittin', a woman my age sharin' her bed with a brat of a kid, let alone a dirty, Limey kid.'

The moon still lingered to light our way when we carried the wash out to the lines in the orchard. Sally started to sniffle and spoke for the first time in weeks. 'Betcha she ain't gonna let us go...' she sobbed.

211

'She don't she goes to jail,' Cathy glowered.

'Ohhhh, makes me feel good just thinkin' about that,' I said with a happy sigh. 'Agnes in handcuffs... But a crust of bread a day ... half a cup of water–'

'Quit dreamin'!' Cathy said. 'And get a move on. The sun's startin' to come up and we still got to wash and wax the kitchen floor.'

We got the floor washed and waxed and, eyes on the clock, sat down to our corn-flakes. Agnes turned the clock face down on the shelf.

Head to one side, eyes twinkling merrily, she watched the boys put their dishes in the sink and head for the door before her voice turned them around and sent them to the barn to sort eggs. She let us girls finish the dishes, wipe off the table and get halfway up the stairs, our fingers busy unhooking our overall bibs as we went, before calling us back down to sweep out her office and straighten the dishes in the cupboard.

'You only got yourselves to blame,' she jeered. 'You'd've done it right the first time 'round you wouldn't be doin' it over. Go get in the tub now, get cleaned up.'

Get in the tub? Get cleaned up? Every cuss word we'd ever heard hovered on our lips.

After one of her most ferocious scrubbings, Agnes braided Cathy's and my wet hair back so severely our eyes were pulled nearly shut in our soap-tight faces. But Sally's hair, damp and tangled as always, still hung over her face.

Finally, we were all lined up outside the screen door, striving to keep our faces blank. Each of us held a lunch bag containing the one tomato sandwich we had made and packed the night before.

Agnes stood inside the screen door. 'No lollygaggin' gettin' home, hear?' she warned. 'I ain't doin' none of your chores while you set all day.'

'Yes, ma'am,' we chorused and turned to run, but before we could take the first step the screen door creaked open. Agnes wasn't through with us yet. She advanced towards us slowly so we walked backwards slowly, our faces thoughtful and serious so she'd know she had our attention.

'I'll want kindlin',' she droned. 'Ironin'll be waitin'. Cows'll need milkin'. Bring them lunch bags home, else no lunch tomorrow...' She stopped walking. Turned back towards the house. The screen door squealed again.

Following Cathy's lead, we continued walking backwards a few more paces and then, at her hissed command, 'Run! Run like hell!' we ran.

We didn't stop till we got to the highway and a good thing we didn't, because we could hear the school bus grinding up our hill as we catapulted out of the woods.

The bus pulled up beside us. Pushing and shoving, falling over each other, yet at the same time anxiously peering back over our shoulders half expecting to see Agnes calling us back, we got on, the driver shut the door and ... we were safe!

Agnes couldn't get at us now with her ironing and her milking and her kindling on account of school buses are for kids. No grown-ups allowed. Tough shit, Agnes!

We stilled our breathing, looked at one another and got the giggles, even Sally. We laughed so hard the driver told us to pipe down and sit down before we fell down.

We each chose a window seat since our stop was the first on the route and that gave us the right to sit any place we felt like.

Andy took his lunch out of its bag, folded the bag with meticulous care, put it in his pocket, and then, with a smirk, devoured his sandwich in a few bites. Thinking, heck, why not, the rest of us did the same.

Then, like animals let out of their cages after years of captivity, and ignoring the shouts of the driver to sit down, we scurried from seat to seat around that bus as if we owned it, marvelling at our ability to sit, to move, to talk, without the usual, ever-present need of sidelong glances from beneath lowered lashes to check the whereabouts of Agnes and her thumping knuckles.

We kept up our outrageous behaviour

until the bus stopped to pick up other kids, when we quieted down and watched them board. What we saw would have silenced us girls anyway, for we were not prepared for the unexpected, new-school-year display of finery worn by all the other girls. Finery that had us sucking in our breath with envy.

We saw crisp new dresses with flounced petticoats peeking out below and shiny new shoes and embroidered socks. We saw rings on fingers and lockets around throats and shiny curls tied back with satin ribbons every colour of the rainbow.

We saw something else, too. We saw the wearers of all that finery looking us over with barely concealed contempt before turning away to whisper and nudge and giggle among themselves.

And there was more. We quickly saw that even though the bus was filling up, all the kids – boys and girls alike would rather cram three to a seat than sit beside any of us.

We sank ever lower in our seats staring at the floor, frowning, because we knew only too well how poor and shabby we looked and frowns helped cover the shame we felt and the tears behind our eyes.

We didn't know it that first day, but on that bus and in that school, we were to remain forever individually anonymous, known only as the Slater kids.

'You've seen one, you've seen 'em all,' the

215

kids shrugged among themselves. 'What they need names for?'

'Those Slater kids stink like a barnyard,' was a never-ending complaint heard by our teachers. 'I don't want to sit next to him/her.'

'Too bad,' the teachers always replied. 'You will sit where I tell you.'

Cathy didn't care what they said. 'Don't make me no never mind,' she'd say. 'I ain't got nothin' to say to none of 'em anyways. Talkin' to them's like talkin' to Sally, a waste of my good time. Time I'd sooner use lookin' for food.'

She didn't even care that the kids called us pigs and made oinking noises when we were near. 'Let 'em call us what they want,' she said. 'We don't eat, we don't get to grow up.'

We earned the 'pig' title because at recess we were the first kids out the door to the playground, not to join in games or giggle and play with friends, but to pick through trash cans overflowing with all kinds of food from the day before. Food the other kids threw away. When we were through scavenging them, we prowled the gritty playground looking for food that had been tasted and spat out because whoever had it first hadn't liked the taste. We never could get over the number of finicky eaters in that school or the amount of food they threw away every day. Good food.

Lunchtime was different. At lunchtime we

could choose between going out to the playground and looking through the lunch refuse, or staying inside to see if anything fell off the candy wagon. The candy wagon was a big wooden trolley with many shelves, each one laden with candy. 'More candy even than Bill's got in his store,' Danny marvelled.

At lunchtime the principal, with great ceremony and jangling of keys, unlocked the door to the hall closet where the wagon was kept. Self-important monitors then pushed it out to the centre of the hall and sold candy to the kids who had money. We Slater kids always raised our hands when our teachers picked new candy-wagon monitors for the week but we were never chosen and, somehow, we knew we never would be.

The reason for hanging around the candy wagon was because there were always kids buying more than they could carry, dropping some, and being in too big a hurry to get outside to stop and pick up what hit the floor.

Then there were others, adventurous types, who'd buy something they'd never tasted before. We only had to watch their faces at the first bite to know if they liked it. If they didn't and we were fast enough, we could catch it before it hit the trash can.

One unforgettable day I found a quarter in the gritty, grey dust of the playground. It had chewing gum stuck to one side of it and was so black with dust and dirt it almost didn't look like a quarter but after I picked off the gum and spat on it and rubbed it hard on the hem of Betty's dress, I saw it really was. I knew if I ran fast enough I could get to the candy wagon before the bell rang and the monitors shut it down.

I felt like a different person – an important one – standing in line with a whole quarter in my hand even though I knew the kids in front and back of me were laughing and whispering about me. Let 'em laugh all they want, I thought. Don't make me no never mind. I'll be the one doin' the laughin' when they see me buy a whole quarter's worth of candy!

Then I changed my mind and decided I'd just buy a couple pieces so I'd get change and could get in line other days.

The trouble with that idea was, where could I hide the change? Couldn't leave it in my desk. Couldn't take it home, either. I was just thinking I'd keep it in my shoes, then bury it someplace the first time Agnes sent me outside alone, when the principal came walking by.

She stopped as though she couldn't believe her eyes when she saw me. What? A Slater kid in the candy line? She couldn't mind her own business either. 'You've got money, uh ... Miss Slater?' she asked.

'Yes, ma'am!'

'Really? Where did you get it?'

'I ... I found it, ma'am. On the playground.'

'On the playground? Let me see.'

I opened my fist.

The principal gasped, 'A quarter! A quarter's not candy money, child. It's lunch money! That means some poor child here is going hungry! And you were going to spend it all on candy? Shame on you! You know the rules about finding things on the playground. You should have turned it in at the office.'

She helped herself to my quarter, that heartless bitch. 'Come see me at the end of the week, find out if anybody's come by asking for it,' she said. 'If not, you can have it back.'

I bit my lip not to cry, seeing my quarter walk away like that. And it wasn't just because I had to get out of the line and all the kids were laughing at me. It was because the bell was ringing and I wouldn't have time to hunt the playground and I hadn't found anything at recess and I hadn't eaten anything since I ate my lunch sandwich on the bus that morning and I was HUNGRY!

On the way home that day, I told Cathy I was going to go see the principal at the end of the week and get my quarter back.

'You want her writin' notes home to Agnes, maybe callin' her up on the phone, the both of them tellin' the other lies, go on ahead,' Cathy said. 'It was me, I'd let her keep the damn quarter.'

I did. I let it go. But every time I felt hungry, and that was every minute of every day, I'd think about that quarter and wish I hadn't listened to Cathy but gone and got it. I promised myself I would one day. Maybe when I turned nine.

There was a sleepy-eyed kid in my class named Billy and one day I saw him getting ready to get on the bus to go home still carrying his lunch bag. His full lunch bag.

'Billy,' I said. 'Why – how come – you never ate your lunch?'

'I used my milk money to buy candy and ate that instead.'

'Yeah? So ... what you gonna do with all that food, Billy?'

Billy took aim and tossed his lunch bag in a nearby trash can.

'That's what,' he said.

I just had time to snatch it out before the bus left. He had three whole sandwiches all to himself! Bologna sandwiches. All we ever got was sliced tomatoes that made the bread go soggy five minutes after they were put to-gether. Billy's sandwiches tasted better than any I could remember. Even better than my previous favourite, the long-ago, egg-and-watercress sandwiches my mother used to make.

After that magical day, I got Billy's bologna sandwiches every day. One day I asked him,

'How about you give me your sandwiches at lunchtime, huh, Billy? That way I won't have to go huntin' around in trash cans.'

Billy thought about that, yawned, and decided against it. 'What happens if I get hungry and want it myself?' he asked. 'Then what?'

Before I started getting Billy's sandwiches the worst days at school were the days it rained and we couldn't hunt for food outside. But after Billy, we didn't care. If it rained I shared his lunch with the others on the bus going home. I gave them each a half and kept a whole one for myself.

After supper the second day of school Agnes got out the butter churn and handed it to Cathy. 'Get busy,' she said. 'The Old Man took a couple extra orders today. Needs to take 'em in in the morning. Sarah, want you and Sally sortin' eggs. Need a couple dozen.'

'But...' I stammered, 'I got ... we got ... homework. Lots and lots of homework.'

'That right? They pay you to do home-work?'

'Uh ... no, ma'am. Well, maybe. Kind of. I could get an A-plus.'

'A-plus's ain't gonna get me out of here, eggs and butter will.' Agnes reached for the strap, slapped it across the table. 'Get busy!'

'That's what you get laughin' at me 'cause I was doin' my homework on the bus goin' home,' Cathy said when we were muttering to each other under the drone of the rosary that night and I was worrying about not having done my homework.

'Wasn't just me laughin',' I said. 'Whole bus was laughin'. You looked a sight kneelin' on the floor with your books spread out on the seat in front of you.'

'Got it all done, though,' Cathy said. And I knew she had a smirk on her face.

'Guess I'll just do mine on the bus goin' in, then.'

'Goin' home's better,' Cathy said. 'That way you got the mornin' to finish up if you don't get it all done.'

Cathy was right. Worked better that way.

Just as nobody was willing to pay Agnes for homework time, nobody was willing to pay her to sign the many papers we brought home from school; papers that required her signature as proof they had been seen by her.

'You'd think them fool women'd know by now I got five homeless brats to look out for as well as a farm to run,' she would fume. 'Jesus, I start in signin' for one, I'll be signin' for five, wastin' my good time and yours while them thievin' squirrels run off with every acorn on the place. Acorns I need to fatten up my hogs.

'More pounds I put on them porkers,' she elaborated, 'more money I get to put in my pockets and the sooner I get out of this

222

dump. Go tell that to your teachers.'

Cathy and I figured that if we hurried through our homework on the bus we'd have time to practise Agnes' signature and when we got good at it, we'd sign not just our own but Sally's papers as well.

Worked like a charm. Or so we thought...

Agnes actually went with us the first time she sent us out to pick up acorns. 'If it means leavin' my rocker and Helen Trent on the radio and goin' out in the freezing cold to make sure you go deep in the woods where the acorns are thickest, then better believe that's what I'm gonna do,' she said. And she warned us, 'Don't try comin' back till them buckets is full, neither. Anybody does, the hogs get their supper.'

After she left to go back to Helen Trent and we'd been at it for what felt like a week with still only about a quarter of a bucket apiece, I asked Cathy, 'How many acorns you figure it takes to fill a bucket?'

'S'gotta be higher than even God can count,' Cathy sighed. 'And it ain't just ours we got to fill, it's Sally's, too. Look a-there – all this time and she ain't got but a couple handfuls.'

It didn't matter how much we threatened Sally to hurry up and fill her bucket. Every day we had to dump some of our acorns in her bucket to get it halfway full even though it meant we came up short in our own.

But we had quickly learned that if we filled the buckets to the brim as Agnes wanted – the buckets being empty five-gallon paint cans – they were too heavy to even lift, so why not share?

Our method of getting those stupendously heavy buckets from the woods to the hog pens was harder to figure but we learned that tilting them just a little and then rolling them at a sideways angle worked best, even though it meant we lost acorns at every step.

A harder problem to solve – and one we never satisfactorily did – was how to walk while rolling those buckets. It didn't matter whether we walked sideways, frontways, or in-between ways, our legs always got battered and bruised from ankles to knees.

It would almost always be dark before we made it back to the house and there were many days when we saw exactly what Agnes had threatened – our suppers floating on top of the hog slops.

'I told you you didn't move it the hogs'd get your suppers!' Agnes gloated. 'You shoulda listened. Get over to the sink now, wash them dishes.'

Waiting until we heard the rumble of the rocker, we'd dive for the slop bucket.

'Looks like the kids at school is right, don't it?' Cathy muttered, spitting out coffee grounds as we scooped out what we could of our suppers. 'Us eatin' like hogs, I mean. So what? Leastways we're eatin'.'

THIRTEEN

The first teacher I had in that American school was called Miss Stacey and I admired her more than any other adult I'd met so far in my life. For one thing she wasn't a nun. And for another she was both nice and pretty, a combination that was new to me. Miss Stacey smiled often, never raised her voice, wore pretty clothes, smelled like roses and when she walked up and down the aisles between the desks, there was a nice swishing sound so you always knew when she was coming down the aisle behind you.

Whenever I was by myself, either picking up acorns or going to the store, I got in the habit of imagining what it would be like to live in Miss Stacey's house and I'd pretend I did.

In those lovingly wrought fantasies, I had a pretty room with a bed to myself, closets full of cute clothes, sparkling jewellery, long, blonde, curly hair, and more pairs of shoes than I had time to wear.

I helped Miss Stacey with her housework

– not because I had to but because it was fun and I felt like it – and she always said, 'If I wasn't seeing it with my own eyes, I wouldn't believe a little kid your age could clean so good.'

She'd have believed it only too well had she ever seen Agnes with her strap going after Cathy and me when we were cleaning. But I didn't want to even mention Agnes' name to Miss Stacey and I never did.

Every day Miss Stacey would tell the class what she said to her dog and cat and what they said back to her. I made up my mind then and there that if I couldn't go live with her the way I was – like a kid, I mean – then I'd be happy to go be her dog or cat.

Miss Stacey didn't have a husband and I thought that was real smart of her. The way I saw it, husbands were the same as fathers and with the two jerks I'd had so far, I'd made up my mind I wouldn't have one either. No, sir-ee! Not me!

One day Miss Stacey said, 'Sarah, every once in a while I catch a word or two of your British accent and it's just as cute as can be. But lately I've noticed you using some very bad grammar and you're picking up a lot of slang. You need to watch that else what are your parents going to think when you get back home?

'Come on up here now and read the words on the blackboard to the class, honey,' she continued, 'and try to pronounce them the way you were taught in England.'

I moved reluctantly, thinking, Oh, brother, now how am I supposed to remember the way I was taught in England? And how come I can't just read from my desk instead of up front where every kid in the class will get the giggles staring at Betty's too-big, ugly dress and Danny's disgusting shoes?

Then I remembered I didn't have to worry about the kids making fun of me anymore. They didn't dare. Not since Halloween when they were putting on their costumes for the parade and one of the boys called out, 'How come you're not putting on your costume, Sarah?'

Before I could think of a good lie or a way to tell him I didn't have one without turning red, the class comedian called out, 'She don't need a costume on account of she's already wearing it. Lookit! She's a scarecrow!'

I couldn't think of anything smart to say back to that either and just when I thought my head would hit my desk from shame, I heard the comforting sound of Miss Stacey swishing towards me and her voice saying, 'Sarah isn't wearing a costume today because as a guest in our country, I asked her if she'd do us the honour of helping me judge the costumes. Sarah was kind enough to consent and, of course, judges are not allowed to wear costumes.'

Taking me by the hand she led me to the front of the class and that was the end of the jeers.

The other kids had to walk round and round the classroom while Miss Stacey and I studied their costumes, fronts and backs. We agreed that being a judge and choosing the best or most original costume was not as easy as it looked. Once we reached a decision and the judging was over, I had a fine time at the party. It was as if standing up at the front of the class as a 'guest in our country' made the kids see me in a different way and they each gave me a piece of their candy as though I was as important as Miss Stacey.

Going home on the bus that Halloween day I told Cathy I'd been thinking it over and had decided Miss Stacey wasn't like other grown-ups.

'I can tell she likes me a lot and I've about decided to tell her about Agnes,' I began. 'I bet she'll believe me and if I can't go live with her, maybe she'll help me find someone just as nice. She might could even find a place for all of us.'

Cathy looked at me like she always did and said, 'Go on ahead. Just don't come bawling to me when Agnes gets all her kids-in-uniform pictures off the piano and lines 'em up on the kitchen table and Miss Stacey wants to know how come you told all those terrible lies about such a fine, upstanding woman.'

Once again, I decided I wouldn't talk to Miss Stacey after all. At least not for a while.

One miserable day at school all the kids were kept in from both recess and lunch because of lightning and thunder. To add to our – 'our' meaning the Slater kids' – misery, Billy was absent for the first time ever and we were beside ourselves with hunger. Going home on the bus the rain started coming down harder than ever and if it hadn't been for our hunger, we'd have liked to stay on that warm, dry bus forever, but the driver said, 'Last stop! Out you get!'

We tumbled out into puddles and mud and right away were soaking wet and freezing cold and all we could think about was going out hunting for acorns with maybe no supper when we got back. We came out of the woods in a miserable, stumbling huddle and nearly fell over a truck parked at the fence.

'Now what's she got going on?' Danny growled.

Heads down against the rain, we were nearly at the kitchen door when Danny gasped, 'Jesus! Take a look over there! In the orchard!'

We looked and saw two men, their clothes slick with caked, blackened blood, working over the hogs. The dead hogs. Every last one of them cut in half and hanging upside down by their chained back feet from the branches of trees where they looked twice as big as when they were alive and standing on those feet.

'You gonna stand there all day gawkin'?' Agnes hollered from the kitchen. Through the screen we saw her, a big knife in her hand, chopping at a mountain of raw meat that oozed and bled all over the table and puddled on the floor around her feet.

'You boys leave the milkin' till later,' Agnes called. 'Go help them men. Fools shoulda been long gone. Just spreadin' it out so's I'll have to pay 'em extra is what they're doin'. You girls get in here, get changed. Don't need no more acorns. You got to get this here meat packed away.'

'There goes supper,' Cathy muttered.

It took us a full week of staying up late every night, plus a weekend, to cut and grind and salt and smoke the one gigantic hog Agnes kept back for her own use.

And there went many more suppers.

When we were finally finished and everything was stored away in the cellar, Agnes said, 'That's the end of hogs on this farm, boy! I ain't never puttin' myself through another week like this 'un. Feel like I could sleep for a week. Would, too, if I didn't have you pack of no-count brats to drive me crazy.

'Made more'n I expected, though,' she rambled on. 'Folks at Wally's work can't get enough of my bacon and sausage. Might could be I'll get out of this dump sooner'n later.'

Agnes wasn't the only one who could have slept for a week. We kids could, too. And we did. We slept on the bus and in class and some days we thought we fell asleep standing up but if we had we'd have surely fallen over.

Miss Stacey roused me one morning. 'Sarah, honey! Sarah!' I woke to find her shaking my shoulder and I could hear the bell ringing. What I wasn't sure about was which bell it was. Recess? Lunch? Dismissal?

Miss Stacey said, 'Sarah, honey, I want you to stay behind from recess just for a minute. It's time you and I had a little talk.'

The other kids were looking at me sideways and rolling their eyes and I knew I must have said or done something dumb while I was asleep or why was Miss Stacey keeping me in?

Miss Stacey waited till we had the room to ourselves and then shut the door and told me to come up to her desk.

Dragging my feet, I made my way to the front of the room where Miss Stacey put her arm around my shoulders and said, 'Sarah, honey, I want you to tell me if anything's wrong. Your face is white as a sheet lately and every time I look your way, you're sleeping! Is there anything I can do to help?'

Miss Stacey's voice was so soft and kind,

her look so caring, her arm a warm comfort on my shoulders, that my eyes filled and my throat grew such a lump I couldn't say a word.

'Is there a reason you're so tired and not handing in your homework anymore?' Miss Stacey went on in the same gentle way. 'And maybe you could tell me why you sign the notes I send home with you? The ones intended for your foster mother's signature.'

Oh, Jesus! She knew it was me signing the notes! Oh, God! Oh, shit! I managed to swallow the lump and said, 'It's because – it's on account of – Ag– Mrs Slater. She won't sign 'em...'

'Them, Sarah,' Miss Stacey corrected, 'Not "'em". Does she say why not?'

'She ... she says she ain't got – hasn't got ... doesn't have time to read 'em – them – all. Just too many kids... Too many notes...'

Miss Stacey frowned, 'I see. Tell me, is she – Mrs Slater, that is – is she good to you?'

I stopped looking down at the floor and looked up instead because I suddenly knew – never mind what Cathy said about Agnes' kids' pictures lined up on the kitchen table – that I could tell Miss Stacey everything there was to tell about Agnes without being called a liar. And I knew no matter what I said, Miss Stacey would listen till I finished. I took a deep breath to begin and that's when I noticed she was leaning towards me, sniffing, a look of disgust on her face.

'Sarah ... honey...' she faltered, 'Your hair... Why, it smells just awful. What is it?'

I stepped back so fast Miss Stacey's arm fell off my shoulder. The kind, sweet lady I'd imagined Miss Stacey to be would never say a thing like that. Never. If she didn't like the way my hair smelled, why, she'd just go ahead and wash it for me.

'I... It's from the hogs,' I stammered. 'I mean ... you know, the smoke from the hogs. It got in everythin'.'

Miss Stacey frowned. She didn't understand.

I tried again. 'Ag – um... Mrs Slater had some men come out and kill the hogs. We been saltin' 'em. Grindin' 'em. Smokin' 'em. It's the smell from all that that got into everythin', includin', even, my hair.'

Miss Stacey's head went back and she had a good laugh. 'Ah!' she exclaimed. 'The smells of autumn! Of course! I guess I was worrying needlessly, wasn't I? Sarah, do you know how lucky you are to live on a farm? Do you have any idea of the price of bacon these days?'

She stood up and, her arm back around my shoulders, walked me to the door. 'I'm glad we had this little talk, honey. I won't worry about you anymore and I do understand about the homework and the notes. Mrs Slater must be the busiest woman in the county right now. Run along out and play now. There's still a few more minutes of recess left before the bell rings.'

My admiration for Miss Stacey in permanent ruins, I wanted to scream in her face, 'Not enough minutes for me to find somethin' to eat, there ain't, you dumb bitch!'

Instead, I turned and ran down the empty hallway and crashed out the back door to the playground.

A crowd of kids from my class were standing by, waiting for me. All talking at once, they called out:

'She give you a lickin', Sarah?'

'She tell you go home, take a bath?'

'She tell you, you stink?'

I pushed past them to the nearest trash can where I saw an apple with only one bite missing. I grabbed it and took the biggest bite I could get my mouth around.

One kid said, 'Oink! Oink!'

Another, 'Look at the pig!'

Another, 'Here, pig! Pig! Pig! Pig!'

I didn't care. Didn't make me no never mind. Besides, I'd just thought about something I'd been too tired to think about before: with the hogs gone there wasn't a slop bucket beside the stove anymore so where was old Agnes gonna throw our suppers now, huh?

For a time after the hog killing, Agnes kept on taking her naps up in Betty's room. But there was no heat up there and with the days getting colder it wasn't long before she moved back downstairs to her rocker beside the range.

Finding her rocking there one particular day when we came in from school I un-expectedly heard my voice asking, 'Bein' we don't need acorns no more, ma'am, is it OK if we do homework tonight? Please, ma'am.'

Agnes came out of her chair and had me by the shoulders so fast we both hit the wall. 'No, it ain't all right you do your homework, Miss Queen of England! You're here to do my work. Cathy, take her and show her what bagging leaves is all about. There's a good half hour yet before dark.'

Bagging leaves was all about getting a sack and a rake from the barn and going deep in the woods where the fallen leaves were thickest – we all took it as just one more sign of Agnes' growing craziness that she thought nothing on the edge of the woods was ever good enough for anything – and raking up a big pile, taking care not to rake too deep.

'You rake too deep,' Cathy warned, 'your leaves are liable to be wet and mouldy. You bring in any like that, count on Agnes rubbin' 'em in your face.'

When you had a pile as high as yourself, you sat down with your back to it, took your sack and laid it out in front of you and placed a foot in either side of the opening to anchor it. Then you reached back with both arms and scooped the leaves under your bent knees into the sack.

'You need to stand up a couple times 'n shake 'em down good and tight in your sack,' Cathy instructed. 'Not like Sally over there actin' like her sack is full when you can tell from way over here it ain't nowheres near.'

'What's she want leaves for?' I asked, settling myself with my back to my pile and beginning the scooping motion.

'For the cows,' Cathy said, exasperated as always. 'What else?'

'Oh... You mean she's gonna make 'em get fat eatin' dead leaves?'

'I swear you're dumber even than Sally!' Cathy exploded. 'Cows don't eat 'em! They sleep on 'em! In the barn! Come winter! When it's cold! Je-sus!'

'Oh...'

With night falling a little bit earlier every day and the wind picking up, we had to get our leaves bagged quickly so the wind wouldn't blow them away, making us start again.

Then along came the windiest, coldest day of all. So cold it made our teeth chatter and our noses run. Cathy looked up at the sky, let out a kind of moan and said, 'I guess it's comin'.'

She scared me so badly saying those words

that I jumped and looked behind me. 'What?'
I gasped. 'What's comin'?'

'Winter, jerk. What else?'

'How come you have to go make even
winter sound like somethin' real bad?' I complained. 'Winter comes every year in case you
never noticed. It's you the jerk!'

'Yeah? Well, just wait. You'll see.'

It didn't take me long to figure out what
Cathy meant. What she meant was, Agnes
used winter as one more way to torture us.
Just like everything else.

Agnes said, 'Didn't I tell you that mother
of yours was nuts sending you over here with
no leggin's and no gloves and no nothin'
warm? I did, so don't come complainin' to
me about it. Go catch your bus.'

'You want to stay warm you got to do like
the rest of us,' Cathy told me. 'Start in running and don't never stop.'

That worked better for the boys than the
girls. They wore long trousers anyway and
they had the old coats and jackets the Slater
sons had left behind with deep pockets to
put their hands in and collars to turn up to
their ears.

But how were we girls supposed to keep
warm running when we were already where
we needed to be and had to stand around
and wait for the bus? Where are you going to
run then? was what I wanted to know.

Cathy thought she was so smart but she

couldn't answer that and had to do the same as Sally and me: dump her books down by the side of the road, try and squeeze her frozen hands into opposite jacket sleeves and then squat so her jacket came down and covered her bare legs.

When a person is slowly freezing to death, it's as if they shrivel up and go inside themselves somewhere and don't see what's going on around them. But once they warm up a little, they start noticing things again. What caught the attention and admiration of all us Slater kids those bitter winter days were the snow suits and fur-lined gloves, the wool caps and scarves and earmuffs and boots everyone else on the bus wore. It gave us something else to think about when we were outside doing chores or waiting for the bus: the cupboards full of snow suits and boots and soft, warm clothing we'd buy with the piles of money we'd have when we grew up. After we'd bought all the food and candy bars we could ever eat, naturally.

There was a time when the sound of the recess bell and the lunch bell were the highlight of our days, freeing us as they did to hunt outside for food. But once winter set in, those bells were about as welcome as the sound of Agnes' voice.

The best we could do, Cathy, Sally and I, was squat down as close together as we could get in a corner of the schoolyard next to some high cement steps on one side and the side of the building on the other. There we'd shiver and moan and complain until the bell let us back inside.

We were there one day, Cathy saying she hated winter worse than anything, even Agnes; me saying that even if the other kids were throwing cupcakes and candy bars all over the playground we'd be too cold to go pick 'em up; Sally not saying anything, just whimpering, when we heard a tapping sound on the window above us and, looking up, saw Miss Stacey. She looked worried and waved us to a side door.

'Mercy!' she gasped, letting us in. 'You girls are frozen stiff! Don't you have hats or long trousers or gloves?'

Our chattering teeth wouldn't let us speak but our shaking heads gave her the answer she needed.

After a thoughtful pause, she said, 'I don't see the harm if you all just sneak in the library on real cold days. Only thing is, you'll have to be very quiet and not tell anyone. Can you do that?'

We nodded our heads vigorously. You bet we could!

That library became much more than just a refuge from the bitter cold for us. It became a home. A safe and silent cocoon, where neither adult nor child came to interrupt our blissful perusal of the shelves of books at our disposal; books that opened their covers to our hungry hearts the way food would have filled our shrunken stomachs.

Reading made us forget everything, even Agnes, until the ringing bell brought us back to who and where we really were: cold, hungry, helpless travellers on a journey that seemed to grow more cruel and frightening with every passing day.

Reading books, even looking at picture books, wasn't the least bit interesting to Sally. Entering the library at a brisk pace, quite unlike her usual lumbering shuffle, she'd head straight for the little low table by the radiator, plop herself down, put her head down on her arms, puff out a happy little sigh and go straight to sleep.

Watching her, Cathy said, 'Agnes is right about her being dumber'n dumb. All these books and all she can think to do is sleep!'

I didn't agree with her. I thought Sally slept because she felt safe in the library and, in sleep, didn't have to think about Agnes or the other kids tormenting her. Or about being cold and hungry.

To tell the truth, I often felt ashamed of the way Cathy and I treated her ourselves when we knew the only thing wrong with her was she was still a baby, too little to do the tasks set her. And that by throwing her in the chicken house back in the summer, Agnes had got her stuck in that mindset in a permanent kind of way. We also knew that things had gone from bad to worse for Sally since the day she handed Agnes a note from her teacher.

Whatever was in that note had made Agnes really mad. She read it through once, went and sat in her rocker and read it through a second time, then strode to the range, opened the top, threw in the note and stayed there watching it burn to a black cinder before slamming the lid back down.

'Had to have been about Sally being dirty and all over sores and bruises for Agnes to take on so,' Cathy said.

'More like it was about her not doin' good in school,' I said, 'on account of I heard Agnes talkin' to herself right after she burned that note and she said, "They want a meetin', let 'em come out here'n have one. I'll tell 'em it's not just the one kid needs help with her lessons. Take a good look at the boy, too," I'll say. Kid don't hardly know how to talk, never mind read...'

A day or so later at breakfast, Sally's spoon scraped the bottom of her cereal bowl – just making sure she hadn't missed the last cornflake – and old Agnes was out of her chair and around the table in an instant to push Sally's face down into the bowl.

'Hog!' she yelled. 'That's the last time you're bein' bad for me, girl! Same with this

241

fool brother of yours! I'm keeping the both of you home from school today!'

Cathy let out a little gasp that scared me more than Agnes' yelling and I wondered if she was thinking this might be the day Agnes was going to beat them up so bad neither one would get to grow up.

Agnes turned on us. 'You plannin' on settin' there all day mindin' other folks' business? Git! Go wait on your bus. Cold might put some sense in your heads.'

Later, in the library, watching the wind lick across the top of the snow and fling it against the side of the building, I couldn't even read.

'You s'pose she's got 'em tied up on the back porch with the pepper rags?' I whispered to Cathy. 'In this kind of cold?'

Cathy rubbed her eyes with the heels of her palms and shivered. 'What's scarin' the daylights out of me is, what if she's thrown Sally in with them damn chickens again?'

There were tyre tracks in the snow in front of the fence when we got home that day. We looked at them and we looked at one another wondering, Did she get them hog-killing guys back out again? To kill what? Or was it the cops she called? For Sally and Andy?

Up at the house there were no lights showing, not even in the kitchen, and we took our time getting there, Danny not even going in but straight over to the cabin to change.

In the near dark of the kitchen, Agnes sat rocking tight up against the range, and on the table were the leftovers of one of her company lunches.

She stopped rocking and her face lit up with a big smile when we walked in. Leaning forward, she said, 'I told Bennings a while back there wasn't nothin' for it but to come get that poor little Sally kid on account of the way you two been tormentin' the life out of her to where she didn't know nothin' no more,' she began.

'She didn't like hearin' that, Mrs Bennings. Pa'ticu'ly when I got to tellin' how you took and locked her in the hen house back in the summer and left her I don't know how long with the temperature way up over one hundred degrees.'

Full well Agnes knew we weren't dumb enough to argue but she was looking at us, head to one side, as though she expected us to say something. That was one of the few times we couldn't help her out. Our job right then was to keep our eyes on the floor so she couldn't see how happy we were that Sally wasn't in the hen house or tied up freezing on the side porch. Sally was out of there!

Agnes sighed, ''Course, Bennings had to go take the boy, too. Wouldn't think about splittin' up a brother and a sister so I got you two to thank for leavin' me short-handed... But the three of you to do everythin' and two

243

of you girls. Jesus! How come nothin' ever works out like I want?'

She stood up, pointed to the table, 'Get this food put away and the dishes washed, then go help Danny.'

Out in the barn Danny came out of the shadows, grinning. 'Andy's clothes is gone!' he whooped.

We told him Sally's were, too. 'Bennings took 'em,' we explained. 'And Agnes is sayin' it's on account of us tormentin' her!'

'Man, they're lucky!' Danny sighed. 'Wonder where they're at right now?'

'I sure hope they're not in another home in the country,' I shuddered. Then I brightened. 'Maybe they'll tell Bennings how crazy-mean Agnes is and she'll come get us!' I ventured.

'Yeah,' Cathy sneered. 'Like the way she hurried right over after James left.'

I sagged. That's how come I never thought about James anymore! The dumb creep never did tell anyone to come get me!

Danny scratched his head, 'Man,' he sighed, 'Andy's leavin' means a awful lot of work for just me, my own self. Both cows. Cleanin' out the barn. All them chickens. The eggs. Choppin' the logs and haulin' 'em up to the house. Makes it just me and the Old Man, nights, too...'

He stopped abruptly, as if surprised at what he'd just said. He turned away and we could see the back of his neck and ears turning red.

Cathy dropped the bushel basket she'd just picked up for gathering kindling and planted herself in front of him, hands on her hips, 'What you talkin' about?' she wanted to know. 'What's he do to you, nights?'

Danny was red all over by then and he grabbed up the pitchfork and aimed it at her. 'I never said he did nothin', did I?' he snarled. 'Git! Go get your kindlin'. I got me two cows to bring in and get milked.'

We picked up our baskets, Cathy and I, and ran till we were deep in the woods. When I got my breath back, I asked, 'What did Danny mean back there? About him and the Old Man? Nights?'

'Don't know,' Cathy mumbled, 'but I can guess. Same as what he does to me'n Sally. Only ... don't see how—'

She broke off abruptly and turned towards me, looking as mad at me as Danny had at her.

'Git!' she yelled. 'Go get your damn kindlin'. Don't want to talk about it no more.'

'I was only askin'—'

'Then quit! Figure it out your own self!'

'If I could, I wouldn't need to ask, would I?'

FOURTEEN

With Christmas inching its way towards us with its usual maddening slowness, the school nevertheless began to exude an extra special kind of joy, cheer, and comfort we Slater kids could not get enough of. For, unlike the frigid interior of Agnes' house at a short distance in any direction from the range, and the absence of any kind of frivolous food, ever, the furnaces at school blasted deliciously warm air, while teachers and kids alike brought in a never-ending stream of special holiday cookies and candies for all to share.

Throughout each day, excited chatter centred on what Santa was expected to bring, while snatches of exuberant carols could be heard bursting forth from every classroom. Add to all this that each classroom boasted its own heavily decorated Christmas tree and it's easy to understand why the daily dismissal bell sounded, to our ears, like the tolling of bereavement.

It's easy to understand, too, that while our classmates cheered every page turned on the calendar, thus bringing them closer to their longed-for Christmas vacation, our hearts sank ever lower, knowing that each day brought us closer to our sanctuary closing its doors on us, leaving us face to face with only Agnes, scared to death every time she stopped rocking, or else freezing by inches outside.

To stop ourselves thinking about it, we began work on a new fantasy. In this one we had somehow found a way to live in the school until classes started up again in January. We had the whole place to ourselves and were just as warm as a person could get. We had Christmas trees to look at, library books to read and big, comfy chairs in the teachers' lounge to sleep in.

The only thing we hadn't figured out was what we'd eat after we emptied the candy wagon. We were in the hayloft one Sunday afternoon working on this most important issue when the urgent clangour of the bell interrupted us.

'Je-sus!' Danny yelped, jumping to his feet. 'Will you listen to that. She's ringing that bell fit to bust. What's she want now? It's way too early to start in milkin'.'

Cathy pushed past him. 'One of us has gone and done somethin' wrong. Wasn't me. Best move it 'fore she comes beats the shit out of all of us out here.'

We tumbled out of the barn and ran towards the back door where Agnes, coatless, was still clanging the bell as though permanently attached to it.

'Get in here,' she roared over the noise she was making. 'Danny, go over the cabin, get the Old Man. Tell him … no, I'll tell him. Go on, now, git! Move it!'

While Danny veered off to the cabin, Agnes, Cathy and I entered the kitchen where Agnes, alternating between us, shook us nearly senseless while screaming, 'The Japs has gone and bombed Pearl Harbor! Jesus Christ! All three of my boys is stationed right there. You hear me? My boys is there. They might could be dead! And how about my girl, Betty? Last I heard she was fixin' on being sent out there the end of the month. Godammit, don't stand there with your mouths hangin' open! Say something! We got us a war goin' on.'

She rounded on me again, fists flailing. 'It's all on account of you Goddamn British! Japs seen how easy them Germans has it beatin' you up'n figured they might just as soon come get us.'

The Old Man and Danny came in and Agnes started all over again yelling at her husband to do something. 'Right now! Call the president! Tell him if my boys ain't dead already I want 'em home. Now! And tell him young girls like Betty ain't got no business bein' in the armed services anyways. Least-ways not with a war goin' on, they ain't. An' tell him–'

For the first time since any of us had lived there, we had the unexpected pleasure of seeing the Old Man raise his voice and his fists to Agnes. 'Shut up!' he roared. 'Shut up and let me listen to the radio.'

After we had been sent back out to the barn with instructions not to come near, what puzzled us most was, where in the heck was Japan? And what, for Pete's sake, was a pearl harbor?

'Don't much matter where it's at,' Danny said, sowing the seeds of a new and exciting fantasy, 'What we got to look for is them Japs comin' here'n bombin' us real bad so us kids'll get evacuated to another country. One that's far, far away.'

School the following morning was an entirely different place to the one we had vacated the previous Friday. American flags seemed to have multiplied overnight and taken over the Christmas artwork. Patriotic songs rang out in place of the carols we'd been practising, and saving for war bonds was strongly encouraged.

Talk from teachers soon resonated with phrases like, 'Before the war... When the war is over... When we've defeated the Japs... It's your duty...' And for those careless or stupid enough to break rules, the all-too familiar question from my past: 'Don't you know there's a war on?'

Patriotic fervour ruled with Christmas an

almost forgotten event until the last day of the semester, when Miss Stacey announced to the class that when we came back from the holidays, she was going to have each of us write an essay entitled, Christmas Day at my House. 'That way,' she explained, 'we can stop thinking about this awful war and get to learn about other people's habits and customs.'

I prayed she'd forget about that essay because Cathy had already told me we wouldn't get presents or a turkey to eat and no tree so what was I supposed to write about?

Then I had an idea. 'I know! I'll write about my Christmases in England before the war, like as if they were this one. Wait till the kids hear about that!'

'They're none of them that dumb!' Cathy growled. 'Jesus! You stand up in front of the whole class in those raggedy old clothes and Danny's shoes tellin' about hangin' up your stockin' and velvet party dresses and toys and games and Christmas puddings and Father Christmas, they'll say you're lyin'!'

'It's what you always say we got to do, ain't it? Lie?'

'Yeah ... to adults. They'll believe anything. Not to kids, though. Kids're way too smart.'

When school was 'in session', as Miss Stacey put it, we kids had become wizards at doing our chores fast so we could get them done before school and, likewise, before dark after school.

What we'd never had a chance to learn was how to stretch them the length of a day. After Cathy and I cleared the breakfast table and washed the dishes the first morning of Christmas vacation and were waiting for the day's instructions, Agnes confounded us by saying, 'Don't look at me! Don't 'spect me to read you stories, do you? Go help Danny. Go play. And don't come near this house till I ring the bell. I need to be on the phone findin' out where my kids is at.'

Play? Did she mean fool around with sticks and bats and balls the way the kids at school did at recess? Jesus! We climbed into the hayloft to think it over and almost instantly came up with one of our better ideas.

We'd stay right where we were and make nests out of the bags of leaves! Yeah! That way we'd stay warm and cosy no matter how cold it got outside. We'd sleep as much as we felt like and if we got tired of sleeping we'd tell each other stories. Cathy and I could tell Danny the ones we read in the library and if we ran out of those we'd make up new ones about how we were going to be and what we were going to do to Agnes when we grew up and boy, we'd just have us the best time! And maybe I wouldn't need to write about my English Christmases. Maybe I'd write about this one after all!

'Won't nobody believe this one neither so maybe you'd best just go on and write about them others,' Cathy said. 'Let 'em think what they want.'

Even though Cathy spent a good part of every day in the hayloft assuring Danny and me we wouldn't get any presents, I knew, with a sinking heart, that I would. And I did. It arrived from England on my day to go to the store and even though I played along with Bill's usual dumb routine to get my hands on it, what I felt like saying was, 'Just keep it! It ain't worth getting beat up over! 'Specially not if it's some dumb doll.'

I thought about throwing it away and I thought about hiding it, but I knew my mother would write asking if it arrived safely so there was nothing left to do but think, Jesus Christ! More trouble!

Agnes snatched the package out of my hands and started tearing away the wrapping and string the minute I walked in the kitchen with it. I knew only too well I'd make her mad if I said anything but every once in a while she made me really mad, too, and thinking I was going to get beat up anyway, I went ahead and said what was on my mind.

'Excuse me, ma'am, but that package is s'posed to be for me. Lookit, that's my name on it. And you know somethin' else? Today ain't Christmas day.'

'I can read,' Agnes growled. 'And I already

told you Christmas Day's the same as any other around here. 'Sides, I need to see what-all's inside. Might could be somethin' that'll spoil.'

The brown paper wrapping fell to the floor and Agnes was hard at work on the tissue paper inside when she stopped abruptly and blinked. 'Why ... this here ain't for you a'tall,' she gasped. 'Look-a-here, that's my name, clear as can be, right there.' She tilted the package so I could see and sure enough, her name was written on it.

The tissue paper joined the brown paper on the floor and Agnes was left staring at what she held in her hands: something that looked like a small, puffy, pale-blue pillow with white embroidery all over it.

'What in hell is it?' she spluttered.

I knew exactly what it was and felt like making her figure it out for herself, but I knew she never would. Not if she lived forever. So I told her, 'It's a tea cosy.'

'A tea what-y?'

'A tea cosy. You put it over a teapot to keep the tea warm. There's a slit on one side for the handle to come out and one on the other side for the spout.'

I reached up to put my hands inside to show Agnes what I meant and felt another little package inside. I pulled it out and my name was on it! Faster than I could think, though, Agnes had snatched it and was busy ripping it open. Inside was a little red velvet box. Holding it high out of my reach, she released the catch and then she was gasping, 'Je-sus, them's pearls! Do you beat that? Pearls for a little kid? And a war goin' on.'

She held them up to the light for a better look, then dropped them in her apron pocket. 'No sense a little kid like you lolly-gaggin' around these here woods in pearls,' she said. 'I'll just keep 'em safe with me.'

'But … my mother sent them to me!' I protested. 'Can't I just take a look? Hold 'em? Try 'em on, maybe? Please, ma'am?'

Agnes' eyes narrowed. 'I let you touch 'em, next thing I know they're busted and rollin' every which way across the floor. Run in the parlour now get me my teapot so's I can take a look-see how this fool thing works.'

How I hated her! To punish her I took a good long look at the picture in my head of the torture we'd dreamed up just the day before in the hayloft. The one where we tied her, naked and kneeling, to the porch posts, poured ice-cold water over her, buried her in snow and, laughing at her pleas for mercy, left her to freeze to death.

Feeling better, smiling even, I got the teapot out of the glass-fronted cabinet in the parlour and took it to her. She put the cosy on it but got it on back to front so the handle barely fit through the spout hole. I decided not to tell her. Let her figure it out her own self, was what I thought.

'Well, I'll be damned!' Agnes exclaimed, turning it this way and that. 'It do look right pretty, don't it? Maybe it's not too cold to-morrow night we'll take us a walk to Knittin' 'n give them old hens something else to cackle about bein' they already know about my flag in the parlour window with the four gold stars on it showin' how all four of my kids is in the armed services fightin' for their country.'

She squinted to get a closer look at the embroidery on the cosy. 'You reckon your ma made this? Special for me?'

'Yes, ma'am,' I said, while out of the corner of my eye I watched Cathy holding on to the sink as if she was having a dizzy spell and knew instantly it was because she didn't want us to go Knitting. Especially not with Sally gone. She'd be alone with him!

'That's what we're gonna do then,' Agnes beamed, 'Go knittin'. Let 'em see how I got me a friend takes the time to make me a gift while enemy planes fly right over her head dropping bombs. Don't you know your ma must've worked on this in one of them bomb shelters they got over there? Goin' near blind from the blackout and all, huh?'

'Yes, ma'am.'

It snowed steadily the next day so we couldn't go to the Knitting Bee after all. 'Even if there is a war on, I bet they had some

255

of the best food ever bein' Christmas is so near and all,' I sulked to Cathy when we were in bed.

'Don't talk to me about it,' Cathy said. 'It ain't my fault. Wasn't me made it snow.'

'Bet you would've if you could've,' I said. 'Bet you prayed for it.'

'You can just bet I did!'

After we finished our cornflakes on Christmas morning and washed the dishes, Agnes sent us out to the barn to sort eggs.

'Beats stayin' in alongside her,' Danny reasoned.

It did, but it was wicked-cold and the snow had turned to rain during the night and puddles that smelled like cow poop oozed under the door and collected around our feet. At some point the door creaked open letting in more rain and cold and there stood the Old Man. We wondered had he maybe, just maybe, brought us something? A present? Something to eat? Candy?

'Merry Christmas,' he mumbled and we knew from just looking at him, he hadn't.

We said, 'Merry Christmas, sir,' back to him in a doubtful kind of way.

A long silence ensued broken only by an occasional gust of wind rattling the door and then the Old Man turned away, stuffed his hands in his pockets, and took a slow turn around the barn till he was back at the

256

door. 'Guess I'll be movin' along, then,' he mumbled, his hand on the latch, 'Let you-all get on with your work.'

He stayed standing where he was, though, as if he'd like us to ask him to stay. Or maybe suggest something he could do to make the day go by. But we were too young, too anxious for him to leave, to know what to tell a nasty old man what to do with a day, never mind Christmas Day.

The door crashed shut behind him and then it was each other we were staring at.

'You dumb jerks,' Cathy spat. 'What'd you think? Think he was gonna give you a present? Some candy? Think he was gonna say, "Go get changed, I'm takin' you out for a fine turkey dinner"? I told you we wasn't gettin' nothin'.'

Danny told her to shut her mean old mouth. I did, too. 'Shut your mean old mouth,' I said.

Next thing I knew Cathy's fist landed in my stomach and I was going over backwards into the puddles. I couldn't see a thing down there but by reaching up I could feel around and what I felt was one of her braids dangling as she stooped to look down on me. I grabbed it and pulled on it as hard as I could with both hands.

Cathy screamed and kicked me and Danny yelled, 'The both of you cut it out! You're gonna upset her eggs!'

We got out of the way of her eggs but he should've kept his mouth shut, Danny, because we turned on him and got him on the floor and then none of us knew for sure whose arm or leg or face we were hitting ... biting ... scratching. All we knew was it felt good. Too bad it wasn't Agnes.

We wore ourselves out after a while and stopped, all of us feeling a bit dumb, like, what'd we go and do that for? But soon enough we started talking again and next thing we knew we were laughing our heads off saying that pretty soon the whole dumb day would be over with. Not just for us, but for everyone else. And even the luckiest, warmest, richest kids in school were going to have to wait another whole, long year for Christmas to come back round again. The poor, dumb suckers!

FIFTEEN

Something very unusual happened the day after Christmas. Something so out of the ordinary that in a matter of minutes Agnes went from being the person we feared and despised the most, to someone we didn't recognize or even know how to describe.

Danny said, 'It's like she's gotten reg'lar.

You know, like ... like normal kind of folk.'

'I guess she finally went and got herself in a good mood,' was how I put it.

And Cathy said, 'It's like she's the kind of person everyone who don't know her thinks she is. But watch out! That ugly old witch woman'll come back just as fast as she went away.'

The unbelievable event was that Agnes received a package from one of her sons. Cathy brought it home from the store. I was ironing in the kitchen while keeping an eye on Agnes dozing by the stove, hoping she'd say something crazy in her sleep, when Cathy burst through the door, a grin nearly as big as the package she was carrying, on her face.

Agnes came out of her doze with a start. 'It ain't another one of them Limey tea thingies, is it?' she growled.

'No, ma'am!' Cathy assured her. 'This one here's from Hawaii. Lookit.'

Agnes ripped off the brown paper wrapping and let it fall to the floor, just as she had with my package, and was left holding a big purple box with a gold ribbon on the top. She lifted the lid and inside were more rows of chocolates than any of us had ever seen in one place before.

Agnes let out a shriek of joy and stuffed one in her mouth. 'Don't he beat all, my Hank?' she gloated. 'Thinkin' about his ma

259

and him in the middle of a war with Jap planes flying over his head. Always was a good kid, that one. Go get Danny, let him see what my boy done for me.'

Danny's eyes bulged as big as ours had when he saw all those rows of chocolates and Agnes was so happy she forgot herself and gave us one each before telling Cathy to carry the box into the parlour and set it on the piano.

'I eat but the one a day,' she gloated, 'they might could last me going on one whole entire year!'

Her eyes sparkling behind her glasses, she rubbed her hands together, forgetting she even had a rocking chair.

'Lemme think now,' she began, 'what-all was it I'd set my mind on gettin' done bein' I got you all home another week?'

Her head went back in laughter and we could see the inside of her mouth and teeth streaked with chocolate. 'I'd a mind to send every last one of them kids of mine a box of my homemade goodies. Wanted me a new cement path, too, din't I? It's only fittin' bein' we got a new year comin', ain't it? Thought on sprucin' up them old hog pens, too ... givin' 'em a fresh coat of paint.'

Everything she'd set her mind on, we did.

We cooked and baked and made home-made candies, Agnes digging out old recipes while Cathy and I ran to the store, sometimes three and four times a day, for the extra, expensive ingredients she needed. When her kids' boxes were stuffed, with every spare space filled in with chewing gum and cigarettes, we carried them to the store, Agnes leading the way and Cathy and I choking back giggles at Bill's face when Agnes herself – wearing lipstick, even – walked through the door.

We thinned old paint of every colour, mixed it all together so it turned into a kind of muddy-looking grey and slapped it on the old hog pens. When Agnes saw there was plenty left over, she had us paint the chicken house and when that still didn't use it all up, she told us to give the shit house a coat as well.

'Too bad all that mixin' didn't turn out red or yellow,' Danny said looking at the finished results after Agnes had gone back in the house. 'Would've made the place look a tad bit livelier than this here graveyard she's got goin' on.'

Cathy and I were in the orchard pinning up washing when Agnes and Danny got going on her new cement path, Danny setting up two-by-fours for the frame and Agnes talking and laughing and having such a good time we stopped our pinning and stood behind a flapping sheet to listen.

'Beats me I can't never figure a way to curve them walkways,' Agnes was saying.

'Curves'd be elegant. Anybody seein' curved walkways'd buy this place in a heartbeat, don't you want to bet?'

'Yes, ma'am. They sure would.'

Suddenly, Agnes clapped her hands, 'I've had me a idea,' she exulted. 'Let's zig-zag 'em! That'd make 'em buy, too, huh?'

'You're darn tootin'! Zig-zags'd do it,' Danny agreed, ripping up the boards he'd already laid and resetting them in the direction of Agnes' pointing finger.

The Old Man had a day off and was on his way to the shit house with a day-old newspaper when he saw what was going on. He stopped and scratched his head and Cathy and I stiffened, hoping he wasn't going to say something that would ruin Agnes' happy mood.

'I told you before, Agnes,' he began, 'this ain't the time of year to be pourin' cement. It'll freeze before it sets and then crumble when it thaws. And another thing I told you, you got to lay down chicken wire before you pour and you got to make 'em wider.'

'I don't recall asking your advice, Walter,' Agnes replied in her haughtiest manner. 'Reckon I got the right to do things any way I please around here and you know what pleases me most, Walter? It's hearin' my heels tippy-tap along a cement walkway like I was on a busy sidewalk in town goin' some place important.'

Stepping up onto the path that ran from the side of the house to the barn, she took several little running steps making sure her heels went tippy-tap so he'd know what she meant.

Walter stayed looking disgusted but Agnes was tickled with the noise she was making and, wagging her finger at him in a grotesque imitation of a dance hall stripper, started grinding her hips and singing, 'Don't sit under the apple tree with anyone else but me...'

She broke off to wave us kids forward, 'Come on up here alongside o' me and sing!' she said taking up the refrain again herself. '...Anyone else but me...'

Walter stood watching awhile shaking his head, muttering to himself, and when we stopped singing because we didn't know any more words, Cathy heard what he said. He said, 'This ain't gonna end pretty.' She was surprised he could read Agnes near as good as her.

Cathy and I were cleaning up after lunch when Agnes picked up her coffee cup and stumbled to her rocker and sat down with her eyes shut. Oh, oh! She hadn't been in it for over a week and seeing her there took the smiles off our faces faster than anything else could have. We raced to finish our inside chores and get out of the house.

Agnes saw us scurrying past the office

door and stopped us, asking, 'Where you think you're goin'?'

'To the barn, ma'am, help Danny,' Cathy answered.

'He don't need you for nothin',' she said. 'Want you two cleanin' up my house real good, bein' you'll be back in school Monday. Cathy, you take upstairs. Sarah, you do down, startin' with the parlour. Do 'em good, mind. Windows, floors, polish. Open 'em up. Air 'em out. Just mind you close up good and tight when you get done.'

I much preferred cleaning the parlour than the bedrooms and was happy I got it even though having the windows open made it wicked-cold. I could hear Cathy moving around upstairs and then the sound of the windows going up so I stuck my head out of my open window and called, 'Yoo-hoo,' very softly so Agnes wouldn't hear.

Cathy stuck her head out of her window and I thumbed my nose at her. She thumbed hers back at me and we giggled because it was fun doing something Agnes didn't know about and wouldn't like if she did. Then we got busy with our cleaning.

I always started a room with the dusting first because that's what my mother had taught me. I took all the Slater-kids-in-uniform pictures off the piano. Also a picture of a pretty young girl wearing a flowered hat that Cathy had once told me was Agnes when she was young. I always looked long and hard at that picture but I never could find the Agnes I knew in that girl's laughing face. I took the box of chocolates and the lace runner underneath it off last, then dusted and waxed the piano very carefully before putting everything back exactly the way I found it.

I was just turning away to dust the little table by the front door when I surprised myself by turning back and lifting the lid off the box of chocolates and peeking inside.

Oh, but they looked good! The top layer was almost gone so they weren't going to last a year like Agnes said they would. And how would she ever notice if I took just one? I was so hungry and they smelled so good. My hand hovered ... which one? There came a thump from upstairs and I crammed the lid back on that box so fast my heart nearly stopped beating I'd scared myself so bad. You want to bet Agnes wouldn't notice? 'Course she would. Agnes noticed everything.

I raced through the rest of the dusting, the mopping, the closing of windows, so I could get out of that room fast and shut the door tight on what I had nearly done.

Agnes heard me coming and came through from the kitchen, a mixing bowl cradled in one arm. 'You done in there?' she asked. 'Already?'

'Yes, ma'am.'

'You shut the windows?'

'Yes, ma'am.'

Agnes made a sound like, Humph, and turned back to the kitchen, only to change her mind and go into the parlour instead. She shut the door behind her.

It worried me her doing that and I stayed where I was in the office thinking over every piece of furniture I dusted, the chairs I moved to mop, the windows I closed, and I knew I hadn't missed anything. Still, I jumped when the parlour door opened and Agnes came back out. She still had one arm around the mixing bowl but in her other hand, something I couldn't see because her hand was a fist over whatever was in it. I glanced up at her face then and right away my heart began to race. The old witch woman was back and she was wearing the dreaded smiley face.

She made a motion with her head that meant I was to follow her and, just setting the mixing bowl down on the kitchen table as she passed it by, didn't stop till she got to the range. There she opened her fist and showed me what was inside: a crumpled pile of the little brown paper cups chocolates nestle in when they're in a box.

Puzzled, I looked from them to her face trying to think what she wanted me to make of them. Still smiling her dreamy smile, Agnes lifted the lid off the range and, just her lips moving, counted off the papers as she dropped them, one at a time, into the flames.

'Four,' her lips mouthed. Out loud she said, 'You stole, you et, four of my Hank's chocolates.'

'No!' I gasped, so shocked I jumped backwards and forgot to say 'ma'am'. I repeated myself then, that second time with some indignation, 'No! I never did! I felt like it but I never did! Not-a-one!'

Agnes' smile grew wider, 'You're lyin'!' she crooned. 'I emptied them papers out the box last night. Ain't nobody 'cept you been in there since.'

'I never took 'em, ma'am. I swear! I never did!'

Agnes leaned down so her face was close to mine and, reflecting in her glasses, I could see only the uncovered, leaping flames. 'You're a thief,' she hissed. 'Just like your brother. Only you done broke two commandments: Thou shalt not steal, and Thou shalt not lie.'

Her flaming glasses went from me to the range top and she chuckled. 'Thieves should burn,' she crooned. 'Oh, yeah! Four chocolates, four burns.'

With a sudden lunge, she grabbed my wrist. I threw myself backwards but she was a little behind me and able to clamp the whole of my skinny body between her knees. Her other hand came down then on the back of mine and she slapped it, palm down, onto the searing surface of the range.

'That's one,' she panted. And though I was screaming, calling for Cathy, twisting in pain, she slapped it down a second time. 'I'll teach you to steal from me. You'll learn...'

She let up for an instant and then, as though kneading bread dough, pressed my palm down a third and fourth time onto that roasting, unforgiving range top with the heel of her palm.

Abruptly she let go of me, stepped back to sit in her rocker and I crumpled, howling, to the floor.

'I can't stand the sight of you no more,' she panted. 'Get on upstairs out of my sight.'

More than anything in the world I wanted to get out of her sight but, twisted with pain as I was, I couldn't right myself with the use of only one hand and I wasn't fast enough for her. Coming out of her chair, she pulled me upright and dragged me towards the table where she threw me in a chair.

'Cathy,' she roared, and over the noise of my own agony, I heard Cathy's feet thumping down the stairs and, through my tears, saw her arrive alongside Agnes.

Agnes smiled up at her, hooked her arm around her waist, pulled her close and said, 'Told you she wasn't nothin' but a thief, din't I?' Cathy didn't answer but I knew her head would be nodding.

Agnes leaned towards me pulling Cathy with her. 'Come on now,' she crooned, 'open up that hand, show Cathy what happens to girls that listen to the Devil. Girls that thieve.'

Again, I couldn't straighten myself on the chair quickly enough and in a lunge that sent Cathy flying, Agnes reached across, grabbed my wrist, twisted it, and slammed my hand, palm up, on the table from where it exuded the stench of burnt flesh.

In a moment of stunned silence, all three of us leaned in to stare in shocked disbelief at what no longer resembled a human hand at all, but rather a fragment of some ancient creature dredged up from the floor of a forgotten ocean. It could not lie flat, that hand. The blackened, charred fingers seemed to want to curl in on themselves as if to hide and protect the blisters that were still swelling and growing on the palm. Blood oozed from several joints of the fingers and there was the ugly shine of bone showing through black curls of flesh at the base of others.

Agnes gasped and attempted to stand and the chair she had been sitting in toppled over with a crash. She leaned against the table a moment, head bowed as though she was having a dizzy spell, and then, holding on to the backs of other chairs, pulled herself over to the sink where she stood noisily retching.

In between heaves, she began to mutter to herself. 'I told her over and over she din't watch where she was goin' she'd end up gettin' hurt, din't I? I hadn't caught her like I done, why ... her face'd be all black and burned up too!'

She stared out the window over the sink a while longer, still muttering and nodding to herself, then turned to Cathy. 'Go get me my little pointy scissors,' she said.

'No-o-o-o...'I howled. 'No-o-o-o!'

Agnes ignored me, walked over to the kitchen cabinet and brought out her largest wooden mixing bowl. Filling it with water from the kettle whistling on the back of the range, she slammed it down on the table in front of me and pointing, growled, 'Put your hand in that water.'

I threw myself on the floor. Snarling, Agnes wrestled me back in the chair, forced my grotesque-looking hand into the scalding water and suddenly, in some inexplicable way, I wasn't there anymore. Instead, I seemed to be hovering over the scene, observing what was going on below as if I were watching actors in a play.

From my vantage point, I saw Agnes pressing my hand down in the water, then snatching the scissors from Cathy. I heard Cathy whimpering, saw her trying not to look as Agnes jabbed the blisters and cut away the skin – skin that was white and wrinkled-looking from the steaming water where it wasn't curly black.

Setting aside the scissors, Agnes wiped the

sweat off her forehead with the back of her hand and told Cathy to get butter out of the icebox. Receiving it, she tried spreading it on my raw ugliness with her fingers. When that didn't work, she gave up and used a knife. Cathy was then sent for rags. While Cathy was gone I watched, still from above, the butter melting into the burnt black and red holes on my palm.

Cathy came back and Agnes ripped the rags she had brought into strips and tied them around my hand up to the wrist. And what I couldn't understand – and still don't – was how I could be up on the ceiling watching everything and yet not feel any pain at all, while knowing full well it had to hurt more, and worse, than anything that had ever happened to me before.

Finished with her bandaging, I watched Agnes pull me out of the chair and point me to the stairs. Heard her say 'Git!' Saw me – the kid – stumbling and falling repeatedly as I made my way towards them. Abruptly, Agnes caught up with me, grabbed me from behind, spun me around to face her, said, 'What you gonna tell 'em, folks ask what you done to your hand?'

I didn't know what I was going to tell them and I saw my face blur as Agnes' open hand cracked into it.

'You'll tell 'em you fell on the range, that's what,' Agnes snarled. 'Gonna say you fell over your own damn feet, like always.'

I heard the kid, me, whisper, 'Yes, ma'am,' and, still from above, watched myself, doubled over like a hunchback, stumbling up the stairs. And then, suddenly, I wasn't on the ceiling anymore, but back inside myself, trying to get upstairs away from Agnes, but my hand hurt so fiercely it was as if I'd been burned all over and even the soles of my feet couldn't stand the pain.

Nevertheless, I continued the struggle while a picture drifted into my mind. It was a picture of Agnes, head thrown back in laughter, her tongue and teeth streaked with chocolate.

Somehow, teetering as I went, I reversed my ascent and stumbled backwards until I was once again in front of Agnes where, fighting for breath between sobs, I said, 'Ma'am ... I'd've et them chocolates like you said I done, my mouth ... uh ... my mouth'd be all over chocolate inside and it ain't, lookit,' and I twisted towards her, my mouth open wide and my tongue protruding.

Agnes hauled off and slapped that gaping mouth, yet even while I was falling against the wall, I thought of something else, and it was as though I suddenly had a mouth that did its own talking.

'Ma'am...' it said. 'Bein' you think I'm so bad, can I get to go to the reform school now? Please.'

Agnes' mouth twisted, 'Bad as you are?' she spat. 'Ain't a reform school in the state'd have you!'

SIXTEEN

Within a day or two of Agnes burning my hand or, as Danny put it, 'barbecuing your hand', school re-opened and a short time after that, Cathy's class started to learn about hibernation.

'There's some kinds of animals, see,' she explained to Danny and me as we walked home from the school bus, 'like bears, for one, that, come winter, just take off to a dark place and curl up and go to sleep, not gettin' up to eat or drink or poop, even.'

We were fascinated by this information because ever since the 'barbecue', Agnes, with just a few small differences, seemed to be hibernating.

One of the differences between her and the bears was she didn't have a dark place to sleep, only her rocker in its usual place next to the range. Another, she did eat and go to bed.

But in between, dressed in her robe, three pairs of the Old Man's socks and a heavy blanket over her knees, she stayed, eyes closed and immobile in her rocker, not even going through her box of cut-outs, which still lay on the floor of her office next to where her rocker used to stand. She stopped going outside to the shit house, too, old Agnes, preferring to do her business instead in the pot, which she had Cathy bring in and place in a corner of the office.

Coming in from school, we got in the habit of standing outside the kitchen door and taking in big, deep gulps of air before opening it to the stench of Agnes and her pot: she, unwashed and over-heated; the pot from being where no fresh air could ever get near it.

'Worse'n the barn, the hog pens and the chickens put together,' we'd gag, averting our eyes and arguing fiercely over whose turn it was to empty that disgusting pot in the equally disgusting shit house.

The pot and the stink aside, we hoped Agnes would hibernate forever as, over the ensuing weeks, we developed several interesting new customs, all in our favour. The best was choosing what we wanted to eat for supper from the jars in the cellar and eating as much as we wanted. Second was telling the Old Man we needed money for the store, then buying only half of what was needed so we could get in line at the candy wagon with the change.

An added bonus was doing our homework at the kitchen table after supper – a supper

Agnes always ate – where we quickly learned we could say anything we felt like in front of her. Either she didn't hear, or couldn't, and once the Old Man left for his cabin and his bottle, we aimed murmured insults at Agnes' drowsing head whenever the spirit moved us.

'You're awful ugly, Agnes, know that?'

'Know how come your kids don't never visit, Agnes? 'cause you stink, that's how come.'

'Know what we're fixin' to do for you, Agnes? Gonna build you a nice, hot fire, that's what. Gonna fill the incinerator with newspaper and gasoline and logs – logs that fit just perfect, mind – and throw you in it. That way you'll keep nice and warm.'

For all our new-found freedom, however, we were smart enough not to push our luck. Particularly not since the day Cathy read ahead in her book and found out that bears returned to their normal, waking habits in the spring.

'They wake up and get goin' again, is what they do,' Cathy advised, 'and we can't never tell when old Agnes is gonna snap out of it. We got to be ready, else look out!'

On learning this, we went out of our way to keep up with our chores both inside and outside so that if Agnes should awaken she would find the fire damped, the eggs collected, the cows milked, the beds made, the dishes washed and the floors swept.

The only chore Cathy and I didn't attempt during the hibernation period was the wash. The reasoning behind that was simple: we were too smart to try. How could we, with Agnes and her rocker taking up so much space in the kitchen there was no room to get out the washtubs? An even better reason was what our own past experience had taught us: wet clothes hung out in winter freeze solid to the lines. And where were we supposed to spread stuff out to thaw, huh? Drape it all over Agnes?

'Winter ain't like summer, anyways,' Cathy said. 'It ain't like as if we're out diggin' and weedin' and gettin' dirt all over so if ever Agnes gets around to wakin' up, how's she gonna know if we changed our clothes or not? Same for the bed sheets. How's she gonna know, huh?'

One morning Cathy and I got out of bed and knew right away something was different. We just didn't have time to figure out what it was. Not with having to fix Agnes her coffee and fry the Old Man his eggs, we didn't. Then Danny came in with the milk and said, 'It ain't cold out there no more!'

That's what it was! We weren't shivering!

Cathy looked scared. 'This might could get her up,' she whispered.

We looked over at Agnes in her rocker, dipping bread in her coffee, spilling and dribbling most of it down her robe, and memories of the tentative, fearful way we lived every second of every day before she went into hibernation flooded our minds.

Danny swallowed a noisy swallow and told Cathy she was nuts. 'Take a look,' he said. 'She ain't goin' no place. She'll be right where she's at when we get home, betcha.'

For all his brave words none of us wasted any time over our cornflakes that morning. Just did the dishes, swept the floor, and left for the bus half an hour early.

Cathy got it right and Danny got it wrong, as usual. Agnes was standing at the range cooking when we came in from school. She was wearing her old print dress, her hair was combed and the rocking chair was back in the office, her box of cut-outs open on the floor beside it. Did she even know she went away – hibernated – all that long while, we wondered? Or did she just put down her coffee cup after we left and go up and change as she had in the past? Did she notice the front of her robe stained top to bottom with spilled food? Or all the tangles in her hair? And how about her stinking pot in the corner of the office? Did she wonder how it got there?

Seeing us coming through the door she said, 'Danny, want you down in the barn cleaning up that old cow. Radio says the men in uniform is needin' more beef. Need to get my money out of her 'fore the gov'ment comes wantin' me to feed the army for free. Damn thing ain't giving milk worth a damn anyways. Alls she's doin' is costin' me good money keepin' her fed.'

Danny looked hopeful. 'You mean Suzy, ma'am?'

'You deaf? I said the old cow, didn't I? Suzy's the young cow. I'm expectin' her to give me a calf in a year or two so why'd I want rid of her?'

Danny took a minute to think that over, 'So's the calf won't eat?' he ventured.

Agnes let loose on both sides of his head with the spatula, hot grease flying every which way and we knew for sure her hibernating was over. But good. The only thing left to wonder and worry about then was, what would she be coming up with next?

Plenty.

'Work you-all through a couple more summers is what I intend to do,' she informed us one Saturday after the Old Man had taken off to deliver the chickens. 'Raise and sell more dressed chickens, more eggs. Grow more vegetables. Go on like that a while, get a calf out of that Suzy cow, then sell everythin'. Every last thing. Sell you-all along with the rest if'n I could. Right out from under Walter, too.'

It all sounded like a dream come true to us. She took off and left us ... sold us... Didn't make us no never mind!

278

'She forgets to call Bennings, we'll call her our own selves,' Cathy said. 'That, or find us a place of our own.'

Wait a minute. Find us a place of our own? That didn't sound like the Cathy we knew who always preached that we were too little and too dumb to count. How was she going to work that one out? And what about the Old Man? Did he know she was planning to sell up and move on without him? If he did he gave no sign of it, but kept right on running her 'in town' errands.

Errands at that time of year meant not only delivering dressed chickens and eggs and butter, but bringing back crates of baby chicks and ducks and turkeys from the Farmers' Market in town. Babies that had to stay in boxes behind the range till they were hardy enough to go out in the runs Agnes had had Danny build for them using scrap lumber.

At first sight I thought all those fluffy, yellow baby chicks were the cutest things I ever saw but that didn't last long. In just a couple of days they turned into the big, fat stinking pain in the ass Cathy had foretold. Not only did their boxes have to be cleaned out twice a day, but they needed an electric light bulb over them to keep them warm, a special warm mash, and water given very, very carefully, some of the chicks even requiring us to use an eye dropper.

'You let one drop of water spill on them turkey birds they'll die,' Agnes warned. 'They do, count yourselves dead alongside 'em.'

Water got spilled, two of the turkeys died, we all got black eyes and our teachers wanted to know what we were finding to fall over that week.

The new cement paths outside had crumbled from the cold just as the Old Man had foretold – even the fancy zig-zag one – and we had to shovel them up and dump the heavy, chunky fragments deep in the woods and make new ones, else who in their right mind was going to buy the place?

Along with Agnes, that's all we kids came to think about then, and over our remaining time in captivity: making the place look good. 'On account of she don't get to sell,' Cathy warned, 'we ain't goin' no place.'

Agnes said, 'From now on, I want you planting more vegetables so's I can sell 'em down at the side of the road where the Old Man's bus comes by. You'll need to plough up that whole entire piece of land 'stead of just the one corner we been usin' to make room for 'em.'

'She's crazier'n a June bug,' Danny complained later. 'That piece of land's just too darn big and we're just too darn small. Why, we don't even got a real plough. Just that piece of junk whoever lived here a hundred years back threw out in the woods, knowing

280

it wasn't but a piece of shit even back then. What she needs to do is hire someone. A big, strong guy with a real plough might could do it.'

'How about a big strong guy with a tractor?' Cathy suggested, knowing it would never happen.

'That'd do it,' Danny said, looking like he thought it might.

We did it. Just the three of us.

'We live to be one hundred years old a-piece and work every one of them days, nothing we ever do is gonna be bad as this,' Danny said, trying to start a furrow in the sucking, weed-choked clay.

Taking turns with that rickety plough, its components held together with baling wire, we tugged and pulled and got stuck and fell down and cussed and cried and got blisters on top of blisters, all the while knowing we had to keep our hands away from Agnes' prying eyes else have her calling for her scissors. The little pointy ones.

Agnes couldn't stand to watch us plough and she couldn't stay away either. 'Look at it,' she'd scream to whoever wasn't plough-ing about whoever was. 'Damn fool's been stuck in the one place all morning long and my seedlings wiltin'... Dyin'...'

Eventually we got all her seedlings in the ground. Rows and rows of corn and squash and tomatoes and kale and beans and two kinds of potatoes and other things we didn't even know the names of, every single one of them needing water and weeds pulled away from their roots.

Back when Agnes had her hogs, she liked to go down and lean on their pens after supper and watch them getting fat and talk about the kind of money she was going to make from selling them.

Cathy and I used to live for those times because they got her out of the house for a brief while, as well as sending her back in what could almost be called a good mood to go for her picture-box. Browsing through it she would talk excitedly about having her an all-electric kitchen with a stove where she could set the temperature any place she felt like and not ever have to think about getting up to throw sticks in the range.

'My kids'll come by and visit then, boy!' she'd gloat. 'They get a taste of all the good stuff I'll bake up for 'em in my new oven, better believe they will.'

The last spring of our captivity, it was the crazy cow, Suzy, that Agnes looked at every night after supper.

'That cow and that baby inside of her's gonna make me one rich, happy woman,' she'd gloat. 'Yes, sir!'

Waiting for the school bus, Danny said, 'I

can't hardly stand to milk "that cow" no more. Not just on account of her gettin' meaner and tryin' to run at me and butt me every chance she gets, but on account of Agnes all the time hangin' around sayin', "You better take good care of that cow, boy. Real good care. On account of that calf she's carryin' is my ticket out of here. You wouldn't want to interfere with that now, would you, boy?"

'Better believe I'd like to interfere with that,' Danny daydreamed. 'What I'd like to do is enlist. Only me, I'd go sign up with the Japs so's I could fly over this dump and bomb Agnes and her cow and that calf inside it to a million pieces. Always expectin' she'd be settin' in the shit house with her picture-box when I got here.'

The Old Man took to looking the cow over some evenings after supper, too, and one day he came back in saying, 'There's something real bad wrong with that cow, Agnes, I swear. Meanest damn critter I ever saw. I was you I'd call in that veterinarian guy when her time comes.'

'Mind your business, Walter, and I'll mind mine,' Agnes snapped. 'I ain't spendin' one dime on that fool. I had a dollar for every calf I helped birth when I was a girl, I'd be one rich woman today.'

Coming home from school one day that spring, we found Agnes waiting for us at the edge of the woods. We'd seen her print dress through the spring growth of new leaves from a good way off and groaned, 'Now what?'

But when we got up close we saw she was smiling and, finger to lips as though she had a secret, motioning us to follow her to the barn, where she threw open the door.

There in the dark, leaves stuck all over her, stood Suzy and she was licking the cutest, dearest little baby calf any of us had ever laid eyes on.

Melting with instant love, we ooh'd and aah'd over it until Cathy thought to ask, 'What you fixin' on callin' it, ma'am?'

Agnes looked at her as if she'd never heard anything so dumb in all her born days. 'Call it?' she spluttered. 'Call it anythin' you want. Just take care of it is what-all I care about.'

'Let's call it Primrose,' I suggested. 'They're such soft, sweet little flowers. Just like the calf.'

Agnes snorted. 'This baby ain't gonna be soft and sweet like no primrose for long. It's a bull! He'll be scarin' the pants offa you in a couple months.'

'Let's call him Superman!' Danny suggested. 'Superman's so big and strong he can do anything he wants. He even knows how to fly!'

Agnes' face turned mean. 'Call him anything you want, boy,' she said. 'Just mind no harm comes to him. I'm holdin' you responsible. Any harm comes to him I swear it'll be the last day of your life, count on it.'

Danny was so gullible, he grinned up at her as though he couldn't believe he got to be the one to take care of that cute, wobbly little animal. To him it was an honour that meant he was special, as if Agnes had just granted him every wish he'd ever had in one big package – a package called Superman.

'Yes, ma'am!' he exulted.

He was so excited and happy I even felt a little bit happy for him myself, although generally I thought of him as dumber than dumb. I looked over at Cathy expecting her to be happy for him too, but she wasn't.

She was looking both mad and worried at the same time and rubbing her arms as if she had goose bumps. Was she mad because Danny got something she wanted, I wondered? Or was this one of those times when she suspected things Danny and I never even thought about?

Turned out it was. One of those times Cathy suspected things nobody else thought about, I mean.

SEVENTEEN

From the day of the calf's birth and ever
after, all Danny ever talked about was, 'My
calf. My Superman.'

'It ain't your calf,' Cathy told him repeatedly. 'It's Agnes' calf and she's sellin' it
first chance she gets.'

Danny was oblivious. Waiting for the school
bus he'd tell us, 'There's a real nice patch of
grass growin' down by them old hog pens.
Soon's I get home I'm stakin' Suzy out back
there so my Superman can eat it. He's gonna
love it.'

'Her calf don't eat grass yet,' Cathy reminded him.

'Today might could be the day he starts,'
Danny argued.

Another day he said, 'You seen them crab
apple trees by the hen house bloomin'?
Man, they're pretty. I'm gonna stake Suzy
out that way tomorrow so my Superman
can get a look at 'em. Betcha he loves 'em.'

'Cows don't look at trees like people, dope,'
Cathy sneered.

'Superman ain't a cow, he's a bull. And
he's got eyes, ain't he?'

Agnes told Danny, 'You better mind where

you stake that cow, hear? I don't want that calf takin' off ... gettin' in the vegetables ... tramplin' stuff.'

Back at the bus stop Danny said, 'What did she go say a thing like that for, huh? Superman knows he has to stay near Suzy else he don't get to eat so why'd he run off tramplin' stuff? He's way too smart.'

'Now, maybe,' Cathy said. 'But how about later when he's bigger? How're you gonna make him stay put then?'

'That's a long ways off yet. I'll figure it out before he gets that big,' Danny answered.

It wasn't a long way off, Superman growing bigger. His curiosity seemed to grow along with his size so it didn't much matter where Danny staked Suzy, he wandered away to explore new territory. The moment he was out of her sight, Suzy would start to fuss and bawl and before you knew it, she'd have uprooted her stake and be chasing after him, stake and chain crashing along behind her.

The sound of her thudding hooves and clanking chain terrified Cathy and me and we'd dive for the nearest shelter. It drove Agnes out-of-her-mind crazy. She'd come storming out of the house cussing and screaming about what she was going to do to Danny if any harm came to her animals.

'I swear,' Cathy complained, 'it's gettin' to where there ain't no place safe around here no more with that cow and Agnes – both of them flat-out crazy – chasin' around the place and comin' at you when you ain't expectin' 'em.'

Along came the last day of school and all the kids getting on the bus to go home were acting like wild Indians. All except Cathy and Danny and me who, as always, sat mute and listless wishing school stayed open year round.

The driver climbed in, closed the door, told everybody to sit down and pipe down, then started pulling away from the curb. Cathy turned in her seat and looked back at the school for such a long time I asked her, 'What you lookin' at?'

'Ain't lookin' at nothin' in p'tic'lar,' she answered with a shiver. 'Just lookin' for lookin', is all. And thinkin' how my whole entire life that school's the only place I ever felt safe.'

What did she have to go and say a thing like that for? It scared me half to death. Especially since she was rubbing away at her arms again the way she'd been doing for the last couple months.

'Quit rubbin' at your arms like that,' I glowered. 'How come you're all the time doin' it anyways?'

'I don't know and I can't help it,' she said. 'Just – get a feelin' come over me that makes me all over shivers.'

'What kind of a feelin'?'

Cathy thought a moment before saying, 'It's the kind of feelin' you get when Agnes goes smiley and sends you someplace to wait on her. You hear her feet comin' and your heart starts beatin' real fast on account of you know when she gets to where you're at you're gonna get hurt real bad.'

'That's just plain dumb,' I said, with a scowl. 'How can you feel that way when Agnes ain't even here? She's at the house.'

'That's where we're goin', ain't it?'

I couldn't say a word back. What Cathy just said made my heart pound and my mouth go dry and all I could think was, Oh, Jesus…

'Even with her gettin' us up a hour earlier and sendin' us back out after supper, like she's been doin', I still can't figure how just us three is s'posed to get through all her work,' Cathy went on, rubbing her arms ever more fiercely, 'a whole entire summer and her not do somethin' real, real bad to one of us. 'Specially now we got Superman driving us crazy every minute.'

Every morning while we were still at the breakfast table, Agnes would outline what she wanted done that day. One morning she began her list by saying she wanted eggs. 'Danny,' she said, 'bring 'em up soon's you get done eatin'. You girls get on up do them beds over. They're all over lumps. Sarah, soon's the store opens want you to run by get me some yeast and don't forget to ask for my mail. Cathy, go scrub out that cabin and get rid of all them bottles. Place stinks like a bar. Danny, stake that cow in the orchard. Grass in there's higher'n my eye. How come you don't see that? Don't forget to burn the trash and for Christ's sake, move it! Soon's you get done your chores I want you all in the vegetables. You're lettin' them weeds take over again.'

She paused to rub her forehead. 'I swear, work's gettin' so bad I'm gonna have to give Bennings another call find out how come she ain't found me more kids like I asked for. Go on now, git!'

Given the number and variety of chores we each had before us, it seemed we'd hardly started on the weeds than the bell was ringing for lunch.

Agnes was standing inside the screen door when we got to the house. She nudged the door open with her foot, handed out a small plate of sandwiches and a pitcher of water and said, 'You ain't eatin' in today on account of I ain't feelin' right. Don't want to hear no noise and don't want none of you comin' near. Go eat in the weeds. Pull 'em while you eat.'

Knowing she would be checking on us even if she wasn't feeling right, we did as we were told and pulled weeds while we gulped our sandwiches. But it wasn't long before we slowed down and soon all three of us were taking turns at the pitcher even though by then the water was already so hot we could have boiled potatoes in it.

That day had to have been the hottest and the quietest we'd had so far that summer. So hot and so quiet even the bugs had stopped flying and buzzing.

'Feels like there ain't nobody else alive in this whole entire world today, 'cept us,' I said in almost a whisper.

'There ain't!' Danny said. 'Leastways not outside sweatin' like us. Bet every kid we know from school is right now settin' in front of a fan like Bill's eatin' ice cream and drinkin' ice water!'

Cathy scowled. 'Shut your fool mouth! We don't need pictures like that goin' on in our heads when all we got to look at is more weeds than vegetables and not a speck of shade.'

Danny stood up and, crouching low, started sneaking away.

'Where you think you're goin'?' Cathy asked.

'Gonna take a leak.'

'How come you don't take it here, like always?'

Danny batted his eyelashes. ''Cause that ain't nice!' he simpered. ''Sides, I seen a whole bunch of windfall apples this mornin'

when I was stakin' Suzy out and I'm gonna
get us some. And I'm gonna say "Hi" to my
Superman on account of I ain't had a
chance all day.'

'Go on ahead,' Cathy sneered. 'And when
old Agnes comes by askin' where you're at
I'll tell her Danny felt like gettin' a lickin'
today so he took off to make sure he did.'

'Tell her anythin' you want,' Danny said.
'And if she wants to know more, tell her
good ole Danny Boy had to go for baskets to
haul off the weeds. Ask her how come she
never thought about that? Say, "Jesus, is he
supposed to think of everythin'?"'

Cathy was too mad to say anything back.
Just started pulling weeds as if she was getting paid for it. She slowed down after a
while, though, and I saw that she was frowning as though she was listening to something.
Something I didn't hear.

'What?' I asked. 'What you listenin' at?'

Cathy's frown deepened and her hand
chopped down signalling shut up! And then
she was on her feet and I was, too, and even
though we couldn't hear much more than a
far-away shushing kind of sound, we knew it
meant someone was running our way and
that someone could only be Danny. We knew,
too, he wouldn't be running in that suffocating heat, with Agnes safely in the house,
unless something real bad was going on. In
seconds we saw him and his face was whiter

292

than white paper and his eyes so big and scared-looking we forgot Agnes might be watching and ran to meet him calling, 'What? What?'

Danny was panting so hard he could hardly speak but between gasps he said, 'You gotta come quick! Somethin' real bad's wrong with Superman. He's– We gotta do somethin' 'fore she sees him!'

Cathy and I took off after him while the words were still coming out of his mouth but he'd reminded us about Agnes and even while we ran, I prayed, 'Please, please keep her wherever she's at till we get Superman OK again. Thank you, God. Amen.'

We saw him then, Superman, and forgot all about Agnes. Instead we were gasping, moaning, 'Oh-h-h, no-o-o! What happened, Superman? What's wrong, baby? Oh-h-h-h...'

His front legs were straddled out wide in front of him and his neck was stretched out straight and stiff while long swags of foaming saliva drooled out of both sides of his mouth like cobwebs.

Closer still we saw his eyes were bulging and he was black with sweat. But worst of all, by far, was the noise he was making: a horrible, gasping, wheezing kind of gurgle.

Nearby, Suzy had her chain wrapped around a tree so tight her head was up against the trunk and she was bawling and straining at her collar.

And all we could think to do was ... nothing.

We didn't know what to do. Instead, we busied ourselves patting Superman and kissing him and telling him, 'Don't you worry, baby. Everything's gonna be just fine. It's OK...' All three of us sounding dumber than the most fool adult we'd ever heard.

One of us said he might could need a drink of water and we dived for Suzy's bucket and brought it over and doused his muzzle in it but he didn't drink. Not a drop. Just kept on with that terrible, gasping noise.

We thought Suzy might know how to make him better and we pushed and pulled at her to get her away from the tree but every time we got her a little slack, she bunched herself up to send us flying and wound herself back up tight to the tree again.

'It ain't no use,' Cathy sobbed, 'we got to go get Agnes.'

We stared at her not believing she'd said that, Danny and me and we said, 'Are you nuts? She sees him like this, she'll–'

Cathy said, 'Yeah, she will. But this calf's in real bad trouble. We don't do something right quick, he might even ... he might could die!'

'No-o-o-o!' Danny howled. 'He ain't gonna go die on me! I take real good care of him. He can't!' He looked pleadingly at Cathy and she looked right back at him, hard. He dropped his eyes, 'What'll we tell her?' he mumbled.

'Tell her?' Cathy screeched. 'Jesus! We got to tell her Superman's sick. Real bad sick! We got to tell her she needs to get out here right now get him better.'

'But ... she said we wasn't to come near.'

'Don't matter what she said, we got to get her.'

We crept into the kitchen not letting the screen door squeal, not making any kind of noise at all. And it was so quiet in there, so cool, so dark after the brightness of outdoors that we stood a moment blinking, letting our eyes adjust, while listening for any kind of sound over the noise of ourselves: our pounding hearts, our gasping breath.

Where was she?

Full well we knew she wasn't downstairs. If she was, she'd have been in her rocker. She was lying down in Betty's room, was where she was. Only we were scared to go up there and, our feet making little shushing sounds on the linoleum, we looked for her behind chairs, behind the range, behind every fool thing we could think of so we wouldn't have to.

We were at the bottom of the stairs, then, squinting up into what seemed a blinding tunnel of light, so bright was the sun streaming in the uncurtained landing window. Blinking, we looked away and at one another and then, suddenly, Danny was taking the stairs two at a time and Cathy and I gasped, hearing his fists pounding on the door of Betty's room.

He pounded a long time, that boy. Way longer than he needed to. By then Cathy and I were at the top of the stairs and staring at his back. He'd stopped pounding by then and was standing in a crouched position, his fists clenched at his sides, his head tilted, staring at that closed door as if, more than anything, he'd like to break it down.

And after all the noise he'd just made, everything seemed quieter than quiet had ever been.

We heard the bed springs creak and then Agnes yell, 'Who the hell is it?' her voice so high and so mad it crackled and Cathy and I gasped and grabbed hold of one another.

'It's me, ma'am. Danny.'

Neither the woman nor the boy spoke for a moment, both, it seemed, too mad to talk, then both started yelling at the same time. 'What in hell's gotten into you, boy?'

'It's Superman!'

'I'll get you for this!'

'You gotta come out, ma'am. Right now!'

'Poundin' on that door like you was crazy when you know when I told you–'

'He's sick, ma'am. Real, real sick.'

We heard her feet hit the floor, knew she was heading for the door, but even so we jumped backwards, Danny the furthest, when it opened and she was in front of us, her and her ugly dress seeming, as always, to fill the frame.

'Sick?' she screamed. 'Whad'ya mean, sick? I told you, boy, I warned you! He caught up in somethin'?'

'No, ma'am, he ain't caught up in nothin'. But you need to come out right now. He's pantin' like he ran a real long way and he don't hardly seem able to hold hisself up and—'

Agnes' fist landed on his mouth. 'You got me up for that? Jesus Christ! And my back hurtin' fit to kill. More'n likely he done run a long way. You seen him runnin' around the place since the day he was born, same as me ... God damn you!'

She turned back towards the bed as if she was going to get back on it, one hand rubbing at her lower back. Danny reached out and grabbed that hand.

'Get the hell out there, right now!' he ordered, pointing with his free hand in the direction of the door.

Agnes spun around to face him, her face so shocked it looked frozen. Snatching her hand back, she rubbed it, front and back, on her dress while her breath came in short gasps.

A while longer she stood there, her eyes going from Danny to her bed, before making up her mind. 'Long as I'm up...' she glowered.

Pushing Danny aside, she headed for the stairs and for the first time saw Cathy and me.

'I'll have your hides, messin' here in the house when I told you pull weeds,' she hissed. She kept on going, though, Danny right behind her, expressing his hatred of her by pulling the ugliest face he could think to pull.

The instant Agnes opened the kitchen door she heard Suzy's bawling and hurried her pace. Coming to the end of her previous zig-zag path, she could see into the orchard, see Superman, and what she saw was a lot worse than Danny had described.

For by then the calf's front legs had buckled and he was down on his knees still emitting that terrible, gasping, gurgling sound. Agnes started running in a lumbering, old-lady kind of way, the three of us right behind her, and then she was kneeling beside him and we saw his saliva had turned pink from blood running out of both nostrils.

Agnes grabbed his head and wiped away the saliva with the hem of her dress and peered into his mouth. Seeing nothing unusual in there, she let it go and sat back on her heels, obviously not knowing any more than we did what was wrong with him. She ran her hand along his flank, which was heaving and sweating and brought it back the other way and as she did so her wrist bumped into an object lodged in his throat. An object we had failed to notice.

She probed it with her fingers, then turned to look up at Danny, her face so filled with hatred we all wanted to turn and run and never stop.

'How long you been lollygaggin' around out here while my calf chokes to death?' she asked.

Chokes to death? No! Oh, no!

Danny tried to talk. 'Wasn't long, ma'am,' he stammered. 'Just as soon's I got done eatin' I come down for baskets to haul off the weeds and when I come out the barn I seen him and ... I come got you.'

Agnes reached out and grabbed his ankle, yanked it and Danny sat down so hard all the breath came out of him in a wheezing kind of groan.

'You're lyin', boy,' she said. 'You went and got these girls away from their weeds first.'

She fingered the lump in Superman's throat again. 'It's gotta be a apple,' she muttered.

Again she turned on Danny, 'Goddam you, boy! If I told you once I must've told you a million times not to never, not never, stake these animals in this here orchard, din't I?'

Danny was still trying to get his breath back and was beyond caring about anything

299

anymore and in a wheezing, croaking kind of way, said, 'You told me this mornin' to stake 'em in the orchard, you lyin' bitch! You said grass in here was higher'n your eye.'

Agnes lumbered to her feet, landed a kick in Danny's ribs and whirled on Cathy. 'Looks like you got the skinniest arms, girl,' she said. 'Reach down his throat get aholt of that apple. Pull it out ... push it down ... whichever. Sarah, you and Danny get around back of him, set on him so's he can't move. I'll hold his head up.'

Whimpering, trembling from head to toe in a way that made all her actions seem jerky, Cathy stumbled forward and tried to get her hand in Superman's slobbering, drooling mouth and down his throat while Danny and I did our best to sit on his heaving, tortured flanks. But the calf struggled with such desperate agony that none of us succeeded in our tasks.

'Get the damn thing out,' Agnes roared. 'Pull on it!'

'I ... I ... can't,' Cathy wailed. 'I can't reach in that far.'

'You try, Danny,' Agnes exploded, 'Your arms are longer'n hers. No, wait. We need something longer yet. Go get me some bailin' wire. We can push it down with that.'

Danny looked mutinous. 'I ain't gonna,' he said. 'You stick bailin' wire down his throat you're gonna cut him up real bad inside.'

300

Agnes' head went down and she gasped and we knew she was having yet another dizzy spell and while we watched her sway, our ears filled with the sound of Suzy's bawling and Superman's tortured breathing, and it was all we could do not to yell, 'Get the hell over it, Agnes! Right now!'

Danny's breathing was nearly back to normal by then and he yelled, 'Agnes! Go on up the house right now call up a veterinarian—' He stopped because he saw what Cathy and I saw: the dreamy, smiley look coming over Agnes' face. He moved in closer to her and pointing to the house, again yelled, 'Go call a veterinarian, Agnes, right now!'

Agnes smiled and shook her head.

We all said – screamed – 'Agnes, go call up a veterinarian! You got to else he's gonna die!'

Ignoring us, she looked at her wrist as if she was wearing a watch. 'I need to get a move on,' she muttered. 'I got me a bus to catch. Should've left a while back... Have to kill him is all. I done my best. Danny?'

'Ma'am?'

'Ever killed a calf?'

'No, ma'am.'

'Me, neither. Don't rightly know how. Ain't got no gun.' She shaded her eyes, looked around, saw the axe sticking out of the chopping block and for a second her eyes lit up. She shrugged, letting go of the thought, 'He ain't no chicken and I ain't got the strength,'

301

she said. 'Think you can do it, Danny?'

'No, ma'am.'

'I got it!' she exclaimed suddenly. 'Rats!'

'Rats?'

'Yeah! Must've killed a million in my time. Run get me that box of rat poison I keep in the barn.'

'Ain't no need, ma'am,' Danny said. 'He's near gone. Look.'

'Did I ask you? Cathy, go get me that box.'

Cathy turned and raced towards the barn.

'And bring a stick,' Agnes called after her. 'A big, long stick.'

Tapping her foot impatiently, pulling on her bottom lip, Agnes scowled around the yard. 'I need to get a move on,' she muttered again. 'Wasted damn near my whole entire life here already. Hurry it up, Cathy! Sarah, bring me that bucket of water here.'

She took the bucket of water I handed her and dumped half of it out. 'It's gotta be strong so he goes fast,' she said. 'I ain't got time to wait around on the fool thing dyin'.'

Cathy arrived with the box of rat poison. Agnes snatched it and upended it over the bucket. Instantly we were all coughing and choking on the cloud of livid green dust that exploded upwards in our faces.

Agnes grabbed the stick Cathy held out and stirred wildly at the powdery green mounds floating on the surface of the water. She chuckled, 'Betcha I could kill me a hundred Supermans with this much!' she gloated. Then, 'You girls hold his head up now so's it goes right on down.'

Too scared and too sickened by what Agnes was planning to do other than what we were told, Cathy and I tried to get his head up.

'That ain't gonna do it,' Agnes panted. 'Danny get on round back of him, pull him up on his rear end, get his head up so's it'll go right on down.'

'It ain't gonna go down,' Danny said flatly.

Agnes looked panicked. 'What ain't gonna go down?'

'That there poison. Ain't a fool alive can't see it won't never get past that apple. You'd best just leave him be.'

'I said I could do it all, Danny, and I'm gonna. One way's as good as another. Get his head up now!'

Rigid with hate, Danny stepped forward and worked at getting Superman the way Agnes wanted him.

Letting out a big Ya-hoo! Agnes upended the bucket. A river of green slime slid out. Some went in Superman's mouth, some in his eyes and ears, but most of it splattered on us kids and the ground.

For a nightmarish moment it seemed as if we were all suspended in a haze of green and then Superman must have tasted the bitterness on his tongue, maybe felt it scorching his eyes – it had to have burned – and with the last reflex of his bursting heart, he lunged backwards, taking Cathy and me with him to struggle and roll and howl in the dust next to Agnes' green-splattered shoes.

She stood watching a moment, Agnes, head to one side, while we coughed and gagged and spat, then, tossing bucket and stick aside, clapped her hands, let out another big whoop and hollered, 'I done it! Done every last thing! Don't have to mess with none of it no more. My time has come!'

Her time has come? What time? What did she mean?

Danny and I were on our feet in time to see her hurrying towards the house.

Cathy had a big, bloody gash over her eye where one of Superman's hooves must have caught her as he reeled backwards. She kept one hand cupped over it while rapidly blinking the other eye to clear it of the poison dust that, along with the slime, coated all of us.

And none of us cared about any of it.

What we cared about, what we could not comprehend, nor look away from, was what Agnes had done to our beloved little Superman. Like us, his face was coated in poison dust with deep drifts in his ears and damp, lumpy splotches around his eyes, nose and mouth. His body was grotesquely twisted, his head and neck looking as though they had been put on back to front by some fiendish demon. And his eyes were open. Open yet unseeing. Without doubt and without discussion, we knew he was dead, or nearly so. The flies knew it, too, as they buzzed and gorged on the surface of those orbs.

Danny started heaving great wracking sobs and kept repeating, 'She killed him! On purpose... The crazy old bitch killed him... And then saying I done it?' He began choking and throwing up and what came up was the pitiful little sandwich he had eaten for lunch. Looking at it, it didn't seem possible that that food could still be inside him when it seemed as though he'd eaten it in another life a century earlier. The flies got busy on that, too.

At just about that same moment, Suzy gave another mighty tug on her chain, succeeded at last in uprooting her stake, gave her head a triumphant shake, and took off on one of her galloping rampages through the orchard.

Howling, Cathy and I grabbed hold of one another, yet, even in our individual terror, neither of us could fail to notice that the other's open, screaming mouth looked like a circle of raw meat in an otherwise green face and knew she must look the same.

Cathy's howling brought on a coughing fit and in between hacks she asked, 'Where'd she go? Where's she at...? Agnes?'

Wordlessly, Danny and I pointed to where Agnes could be seen standing, arms akimbo, on the porch. We knew we'd better find a way to capture Suzy and clean ourselves up. Fast.

EIGHTEEN

One evening in the winter after Superman died, Agnes suddenly stomped out of her office and announced: 'I called that Mrs Bennings woman in town and told her to come get you. Told her I couldn't abide bein' around you no more. Said I'd thought with that brat brother of yours gone from the place you'd change but you never have. Never will, as far as I can tell.'

I was too stunned to fully comprehend.

'Bennings said she'd be out first thing in the mornin'. Said there's always some kids just don't know when they're well off, you bein' the worst of 'em.

'Get upstairs now, find that suitcase you brung with you. Fill it up with every last thing you got. Don't want you leaving nothing behind that'll remind me of you and your ugly face.'

I recovered enough from my shock to hear myself ask, 'What about my clothes you took and gave to Cathy? You want me to take them too?'

Cathy was actually still wearing some of my things, now horribly tattered. For some reason, she just didn't seem to grow much.

'They ain't yours no more,' Agnes snarled. 'You done give 'em to Cathy. You take 'em back to England, she won't have nothin' to wear. You want her runnin' around stark naked? Knowin' you, you'd like that, wouldn't ya?'

I wasn't sure what I'd like or what I wouldn't like at that point. And I was terrified to even hope that I was actually going to leave the farm for good.

In the car on our way to New York, Mrs Bennings said, 'I still can't get over your folks expecting you to cross the Atlantic Ocean all by yourself with a war still going on. U-boats ... Jap boats ... everywhere. Sounds crazy to me but that's what they've made up their minds to have you do.

'Just try not to worry,' she continued. 'Remember, James is there already, safe and sound.'

'James? You mean my brother, James?' I yelped coming out of my torpor and sitting up straighter. 'He's in England? I thought he was in a reform school!'

Mrs Bennings gasped and said, 'Now who in the world told you a thing like that? He was never in a reform school, for heaven's sake! He was in a very fine boarding school. And I know for a fact I told Mother Slater he was back home safe. Told her that time I called up to say I was still working on finding her the two new kids she asked for and doing the paperwork on you. Why, he's been home a month gone already. Got to go on an aircraft carrier. Just him and one other kid. How about that?'

I was thinking all that through: Agnes knowing I would be leaving but never mentioning it ... James back in England ... two new kids coming to live – do slave labour, more like – at the farm, when Mrs Bennings went and got mad.

'I can see you're still the same closed-mouth kid you were back when I first brought you out here,' she huffed. 'Lord! I'd think you'd have something to say. Be excited about going back into the loving arms of a family you haven't seen in four years. I know I would! Even though they will have changed.'

She sighed one of her big sighs, 'That's something you've got to expect, Sarah. Just like they'll see you've changed. Lord, what are they going to say when they see what a great big girl you are now? And so Americanized?'

I didn't know and didn't care what they'd say about any of those things. I hadn't thought about them in such a long time I could hardly remember what they looked like. The only clear memory I retained of that part of my life was my father's violent temper.

Mrs Bennings heaved more of her big sighs and said, 'Sarah, it's not doing you any good looking out that rear window like you're doing. There's no going back, you know. The past is the past and a good thing, too, I'd say, with all you've got on your conscience.

'Lord! It's a wonder you can sleep nights the way you and those two others took it into your heads to kill that darling little calf. And with poison of all things! And then saying Mother Slater did it when you know well as I do that calf was her pride and joy. Humph! You might've fooled old man Bill at the store and maybe some others, but you didn't fool me. Not for one minute. I'll never forget about that all of my born days.

'Good thing your folks want you home, is all I can say, else who'd take you? A bad dream is what you two turned out to be. An out-and-out nightmare.'

She dug around in her pocketbook with one hand, meantime letting the car head for the ditch running alongside the road. She got it straightened just in time, pulled a tissue out of her pocketbook and dabbed at her eyes and blew her nose and then, on another deep breath, said, 'Do like I said

309

now and turn around in your seat and face the front. You got to look ahead, Sarah. That's where the future lies for you and me both and that's where we're headed.'

I turned around and faced the front, not because she told me to but in the hope she'd stop her talk, talk, talking. I wasn't looking back from a sense of fondness, heaven only knew. It was more like when you can't stop staring at an accident scene along the road.

Mrs Bennings prodded, 'Sarah, you're not crying, are you? Why ... I do believe you are! What in the world have you got to cry about now? Really!'

NINETEEN

If I'd had a chance to talk, I might have told Bennings that I was crying because now that the unbelievable had happened and I'd gotten over knowing I'd never have to see or speak to Agnes again, my mind had turned to the future, and that future held two new terrors. One was having to get on a boat the size of a skyscraper lying on its side and cross the Atlantic in it while submarines chased after us; the other was coming once again face to face with my father at the end of the journey, for my head had begun teeming

310

with memories, bad memories, of both.

I recalled that small cabin James and I had shared on the journey from England and in retrospect it seemed as though we had spent all our time crying and being violently sea-sick, most often simultaneously. We had had an 'escort' to be sure, a childless woman of middle years who was to keep an eye on us and several other children – of which we were the youngest – and see that we kept ourselves clean, brushed our teeth, changed our under-wear, ate our vegetables, and went to bed when we were told. But her tasks were made somewhat simpler, since we were often too seasick to dress and leave our cabin at all and, some days, a simple rap on our door, fol-lowed by her head peering around it to verify our presence, were all that were required of her.

Mounting the gangplank of the ship going back to England on a frigid December morn-ing in 1944, and accompanied by a middle-aged woman chosen by somebody or other to look after me during the journey, I wondered if I would have to share a small cabin with her and was very relieved to find we were shown to a large cabin containing ten or twelve bunks. It was suggested to me that I take one of the upper bunks and this I did, grateful that for once James was not there to push me down to a lower one.

We had not been on board long when we

were told that the noisy hooting we could hear outside signified that we were departing New York. All of us in the cabin hurried to an upper deck to observe this event. The woman I was travelling with told me to wave goodbye to the country that had been my home for four years but all I could think about was nasty old Agnes and, to my companion's dismay, I accompanied my waves with a lot of ugly faces and sticking my tongue out, while my farewell wishes had to do with her imminent demise.

We were travelling in a convoy of ships and I can only guess now at the number of vessels accompanying us, perhaps twenty, but all the people surrounding me assured me and each other that in their midst we would be very safe from the enemy submarines that still plagued the ocean.

No sooner were we back in our cabin after the farewell than I began to feel the first stirrings of the seasickness that had been such a part of my previous journey and I was disgusted that, in the four years between journeys, I had not outgrown it. For, as best I could recall, it seemed that none of the adults on the previous journey had succumbed to it.

I was particularly unhappy to feel such seasickness as I had really looked forward to being able to eat all the kinds of food that Agnes had never served and now just the thought of any of them made me feel sicker than a dog.

So there I was, back in bed on the third day out and feeling horrible when the loudspeakers blared that we were all to report to the lounge as the captain had an important announcement to make.

I was told to stay in bed but my companion, on returning, told me that our ship was undergoing severe engine trouble and we had to go back to New York for repairs.

Unlike my fellow travellers, I was pleased to hear of our problems as they would give me a little more time away from my father.

'You just don't comprehend,' my companion told me, sourly. 'Surely it's better to face your father than to travel back to New York without a convoy to keep us safe.'

'You mean we have to turn back alone?' I asked.

'Now you've got it,' she replied. 'The submarines can blow us to bits if they feel like it now. Won't be anything there to stop them.'

One way or another, we made it back to New York safely and were told we would be there five days while repairs were made. We could, however, leave the ship every day on shore leave as long as we were back on board by six p.m.

Everybody but me was thrilled and talked about doing their Christmas shopping and browsing the New York department stores.

I didn't have the money to buy so much as

a lollipop so decided not to go, but my cabin mates insisted, and I had a good time with them buying me lots of stuff, both to eat and to wear. I particularly remember seeing what I would have sworn was the real Santa Claus sitting in a department store window, laughing his head off and slapping his knee. But I was told it was just a guy in a Santa suit, which really took the fun out of it.

Our five days were over and we were told we were seaworthy once more and could begin our journey all over again. And that, with a bit of luck, we'd be in England for Christmas. But ... this time there would be no convoy.

Oh, my but that ocean looked awfully big, and awfully grey and awfully cold and lonely. I couldn't help but wonder why there wasn't some adult somewhere who would put a stop to our journey at once. But then, I had already learned that adults are never ready to behave like adults when you really need them to. It's just easier for them to appear helpless, keep their mouths shut, and look the other way, I guess. It made me wonder what kind of an adult I'd be when the time came? A better one than most, I felt sure.

We had lifeboat drill practice sessions every day on our way home and, in the end, I was almost disappointed we didn't have a real attack as I felt very ready to deal with the enemy in whatever shape or form it took.

As it was, the biggest enemy I had to deal with, then and for weeks thereafter, was a case of ferociously itching athlete's foot, picked up, no doubt, from padding around our cabin in my bare feet. After all, it wasn't written anywhere that Agnes had to provide me with slippers.

We had only been at sea a couple of days when some of the ladies took it into their heads that we should put on a ship's concert on our second to last day on board. All those wishing to perform were asked to sign up in the ship's lounge after breakfast the following day and indicate the manner in which they would perform.

Thanking God for not burdening me with any particular talent, I was just helping myself to an extra piece of toast when a woman pounced on me and said she would teach me to sing a song. I assured her I would not and could not sing, but somehow or other, on the night of the concert, I stood alone on the stage and warbled a ridiculous song about a lonely little petunia, during which I had to look very pathetic and pat my heart. I imagined the expression on my face looked angry rather than pathetic but a lot of people clapped anyway.

Finally, we were pulling into the docks at Liverpool (I think it was Liverpool) and I was going to have to get off the ship and go out and act happy about rejoining my family.

I stood for quite a while in the customs shed near my suitcase, looking out fearfully for my father and mother, hoping I'd spot them before they spotted me. I did see them, and by standing sideways and keeping my head mostly turned away from them, I was able to look them over without them having any idea who I was. Studying them thus, I surprised myself by starting to feel sorry for them.

My father looked like just any other old man and not at all the fierce, violent person I had carried in my head for four years. As for my mother, she looked bone tired and was dressed in the same threadbare clothes she had worn before I went away. Her hair had now turned completely white and I could only imagine how ghastly it must have been for her to have had only my father and Hitler as companions through those long, lonely years.

Propelled by my surprising rush of pity for both of them and abandoning my pretence of examining suitcases, I approached them, pleased to realize as I did how much I had grown during my absence. Why, now I was no longer peering up at my father from down around his knees but from mid-chest. And I looked at my mother from almost her neck. I felt confidence surge through me as they finally recognized me, and I gave them a big smile that said, 'I'm back!'

EPILOGUE

When the day arrived that James and I, like spent volcanoes run out of steam, came to the end of our reminiscences, we sat staring at one another in silence for a very long time.

James was the first to speak. 'So...' he said, 'it wasn't just about four years after all, was it? More like our entire bloody lives if you ask me. But ... it's all out now, isn't it? I mean, we didn't forget anything?'

'Nope,' I said. 'We got it all.'

'Wonder what took us so long?' he mused.

'We weren't ready,' I answered. 'Simple as that.'

'Still ... sixty odd years is a hell of a long time.'

'Could have been seventy,' I shrugged.

'You've had the advantage, though,' he said. 'All along, you knew. You were there. I wasn't. Think of the years I've had to wonder.'

'You could have asked,' I said. 'Anytime.'

'You could have mentioned it,' he replied.

'I thought about it once in a while but it wasn't something I wanted to talk about,' I said, 'It's obvious now that neither one of us wanted, or were ready, to bring up any part

317

of it.'

James stood up and pulled on his jacket, 'You did what you had to do and you survived. And I can better understand now why we never discussed it before. Quite simply, we were afraid that if we once prised open the can, we'd never get the lid back on again. Can you believe that after all those years she still haunted us to the degree she has?'

'Yes,' I agreed. 'She's always been there, hasn't she? A part of who we are, really. Maybe now the nightmares will end, too. You know, the one where the old fool calls for her little pointy scissors. The one where—'

James frowned and put his finger to his lips to silence me. 'They won't be back,' he said. 'Trust me. It's all truly behind us now.'

He was right. Agnes, and the nightmares that went along with her, are gone. Gone wherever it is memories go when their time runs out. And, Agnes, it's time now for you to go rest in peace, too. No one, not a single soul, will miss you.

The publishers hope that this book has given you enjoyable reading. Large Print Books are especially designed to be as easy to see and hold as possible. If you wish a complete list of our books please ask at your local library or write directly to:

Magna Large Print Books
Magna House, Long Preston,
Skipton, North Yorkshire.
BD23 4ND